1994

1995

N 1

JAGUAR

JAGUAR

Rebirth of a Legend

KEN CLAYTON

CENTURY

LONDON SYDNEY AUCKLAND JOHANNESBURG

First published in Great Britain in 1988 by
Century Hutchinson Ltd
Brookmount House, 62–65 Chandos Place,
Covent Garden, London WC2N 4NW

Century Hutchinson Australia (Pty) Ltd
89–91 Albion Street, Surry Hills,
New South Wales 2010, Australia

Century Hutchinson New Zealand Ltd
PO Box 40-086, 32–34 View Road, Glenfield,
Auckland 10, New Zealand

Century Hutchinson South Africa (Pty) Ltd
PO Box 337, Bergvlei 2012, South Africa

Photoset in Linotron Times New Roman by
Rowland Phototypesetting Ltd
Bury St Edmunds, Suffolk
Printed and bound in Great Britain by
Mackays of Chatham plc, Chatham, Kent

British Library Cataloguing in Publication Data
Clayton, Ken
Jaguar.
1. Jaguar cars, 1975–1986
I. Title
629′.2′222

ISBN 0-7126-2331-0

To my children, Simon and Nicola and to Cath Neale
(who's always wanted a book dedicated to her.)

Contents

Illustrations

Sir John Egan, Sir William Lyons,
Geoffrey Robinson and Bob Knight

The winning XJR9, Le Mans 1988
and the XJ5.3 coupé, Silverstone 1977

Le Mans 1956 and Goldrush 1984

The old paint shop and cramped
final assembly lines, Browns Lane

XJ40 assembly, Browns Lane

The XJ40 being assessed by potential customers,
and on test in Australia

A J Day at the National Exhibition Centre
and XJ40 press launch, Tucson, Arizona

The XJ6, London Motor Show, Earls Court, 1968
and XJ40 on display at the British Motor Show, 1986

Acknowledgements

Many people have been very generous with their time in explaining the background to the events covered by the book. They are all listed in Appendix 9, along with their relevant job titles. However, I take this opportunity to offer my heartfelt thanks to each of them.

In addition, a number of people have helped with advice, comment and information. Among them, I particularly want to thank Stephen Batiste, Richard Isom, David Oates, Alan Purkiss, Christine Smith and Kelvin Teal. Ian Luckett of Jaguar has been a great help throughout the preparation of the book, while Roger Clinkscales of Jaguar's photographic department was enormously helpful in finding photographs.

Finally, thanks are due to the long-suffering staff of the Society of Motor Manufacturers and Traders for their constant willingness to provide information.

Introduction

Today, Jaguar is seen as a manufacturer of luxury cars that are eminently suitable for company chairmen, but this image has been earned only since the early 1970s. Before the war, SS Cars, as the company was then called, built stylish saloons and sports cars, but it still bought chassis and engines from outside manufacturers. It was not until 1948 that the first engine designed and developed by Jaguar engineers appeared. This was the remarkable XK Series engine, introduced in the XK 120 sports car.

The sporting image was enhanced by successes in motor sport, notably in the Le Mans 24 Hour Race. The company won the race for the first time in 1951; it was the first British winner in 16 years. Such successes, which helped to gain the company world-wide publicity, were a considerable achievement, but perhaps even more remarkable is the number of Jaguar models that have come to be regarded as classics of their type. They include the XK 120 and the two models that followed it: the Mark 2 compact saloon, introduced in 1959; and the E-Type, launched in 1961. All were examples of Jaguar at its best.

Attractive as the company's cars were, however, they tended to be seen as too racy for the establishment. A Jaguar was not quite respectable, even in the 1960s. In those days, a sales manager might have one, but it was definitely not an acceptable car for a finance director. Film makers recognised the Mark 2 saloon as a superb getaway car for bank robbers and underworld hoodlums. Every crime film of the time seems to have involved a chase with the villains racing away in their Mark 2, usually to crash it in a spectacular fashion. The image did not help sales. One man who joined the board of a big company in the mid-1960s recalls that when he was appointed, no director had a Jaguar. A few years later, they all had them.

The change in the way the marque was perceived began with the introduction of the XJ6 saloon in 1968. This car moved Jaguar into a new era of respectability. At the same time, the company kept its reputation for producing "a lot of car for the money". Second-hand values of Jaguars were low enough to make them attractive to people who could never have afforded a new Jaguar. The company was not seen unequivocally as a manufacturer of real luxury cars until the drive for improved quality in the early 1980s.

Jaguar had finally realised that it was selling to very discerning customers at a time when car buyers had become more demanding anyway. It faced up to the fact that people who were prepared to pay four times what it cost to buy an ordinary family saloon, wanted a car that worked. But this acknowledgement of market realities is only one reason for the changes that have occurred at Jaguar since 1980. The company has grown up. It displays a more professional attitude to the business of designing, building and selling cars than it used to. The change has come about rather late. There is little doubt that, had the company been better managed from the 1950s to the early 1980s it would be bigger and more successful today.

The way Jaguar was managed over the 20 years to the launch of the new XJ40 in the autumn of 1986 is the subject of this book. Accounts of the company's cars, of its racing successes and of its earlier history are readily available elsewhere. What no one has explained yet is what happened between 1966 and 1984, when the company again became an independent car maker.

Inevitably, a book such as this raises "what if?" questions. The biggest is the easiest to answer. What if Sir William Lyons had not sold the company to the British Motor Corporation in 1966? The chances are that Jaguar would now be at most a name applied to somebody else's car. It is virtually certain that it would not be an independent company today. By the time Lyons sold it, Jaguar had relied for too long on minimal investment and inadequate manage-ment to be viable in the long term.

Yet Jaguar is a curious entity. Car companies have always tended to produce emotional reactions, and none more so than Jaguar. Over the years, various people have been put into the company to "sort it out", only to become dyed in the wool Jaguar people themselves, manning the barricades with the others. The 20 years leading up to the launch of the XJ40 were traumatic for the company and for the people who worked within it. I have attempted to trace the events of that period as accurately as possible. All the main events are covered, and the recollections of those who were involved are recorded. The research for this book has been fascinating. I hope you find it as interesting to read the result.

Ken Clayton   Tamworth, 1988

CHAPTER 1

The Seeds of Disaster

For half a century, Jaguar's fortunes were largely determined by one man: William Lyons, the company's founder. Lyons was born in Blackpool in 1901. After leaving school at 17, he went to work for Crossley Motors, a vehicle manufacturer in Manchester. It was not long, however, before he returned to Blackpool to work in his father's piano repair business. A spell with the Blackpool retail motor trade followed, first with Jackson Brothers and later with Brown and Mallalieu where Lyons worked as a junior sales-man. Throughout this period, he was a keen motor cyclist, owning both Harley Davidson and Indian motor cycles at various times.

In 1921, he discovered that a new neighbour was building smart motor cycle sidecars. This was William Walmsley, who had begun making sidecars after the First World War. Lyons thought they had considerable sales potential and persuaded Walmsley to go into partnership with him. The original Swallow Sidecar Company was formed on the strength of a £1,000 bank overdraft that was guaranteed by the new partners' fathers. Indeed, Lyon's father had to sign all the papers on his son's behalf: Lyons was not yet 21 when the company was formed in 1922, and so could not sign legally binding contracts.

The new company soon branched out into the manufacture of stylish bodies for small cars, and moved to Coventry in 1928. That brought the company closer to its suppliers and a ready source of skilled labour. The company grew and prospered through the 1920s, and in 1933, Lyons and Walmsley formed SS Cars Ltd. The Swallow business was transferred into the new company. But the partnership between the two men was not to last much longer. In November 1934 Walmsley resigned from the company. Two months later, SS Cars was floated on the Stock Exchange. The company had turned in a profit of £37,645 for the 12 months to

July 31, 1934, and had net assets of £179,857. Lyons retained a majority of the shares and became chairman and managing director.

For 30 years, until well into the 1960s, the company – which changed its name to Jaguar Cars in March 1945 – prospered, and most of the credit was due to Lyons. From the beginning, he was determined to run the business his way, and took decisions without reference to his fellow-directors. There were apparently no board meetings until the mid-1960s. Lyons kept colleagues at a distance. Even those who were with him for years would never be referred to by their first names. Nor was he a man to spend time on social pleasantries. One man who worked closely with him recalls that when Lyons telephoned him for information, the receiver would be put down as soon as he had got what he wanted. Few colleagues appear to have known him socially. He maintained a gulf between business and his private life.

Not surprisingly, Lyons, who died in 1985, is often remembered as an autocrat, who ruled a public company as if it were his own. That is undoubtedly true, yet it is an incomplete picture. He was respected and well liked, not only at Jaguar but throughout the motor industry. Those who worked with him frequently describe him as a gentleman. As one puts it: "Nobody ever spoke badly of Bill." That is a considerable tribute to a man who had the drive and determination to create one of the most prestigious companies in Britain.

He was instinctively parsimonious. "If he had a bucket with a hole in it, he'd mend the hole rather than buy a new bucket," recalls a former colleague. Another declares: "Bill would have bought a second-hand production line if he had thought it would be cheaper." But it is symptomatic of the respect with which Lyons was regarded that neither comment betrays any hint of malice. His "eye for a bargain" was a legacy of his early years in business.

As a car manufacturer Lyons was, above all, a stylist. In creating the body-shape of a new model, he worked after the fashion of a sculptor. Once a small team had fashioned the panels under his direction, he would spend hours looking at the resulting shape from every angle, calling for changes to curves and to highlights. When he felt it was almost right, he would have the mocked-up body taken to his home and placed outside the door. As a former colleague explains, "He used to say that it was no use looking at a car in a studio when people were going to see it outside their front doors." Only when he personally was completely satisfied with it would the shape be passed for manufacture.

Over the years the company produced a series of remarkable cars. The SS100 was its first sports car and has become one of the most sought-after classics of the time. The XK120, announced in 1948, and its successors captured the imagination of post-war Britain as no other cars did. The Jaguar 2.4, which came out in 1955, caused a problem for the company by virtue of its very success. This mid-range saloon was the most successful car that Jaguar had made to date. It was not surpassed in terms of sales volume until the XJ6 was launched 13 years later.

The problem was that the company did not have the space to build enough cars to satisfy the worldwide demand and could not get planning approval to extend the existing factory. The government of the day was encouraging companies to build factories in depressed areas. Lyons (who received a knighthood in 1956) foresaw difficulties in having one factory in Coventry and another in Scotland or Liverpool. He decided against expanding by that route, opting instead for what seemed an altogether more satisfactory solution: Jaguar bought the Daimler company, which made cars and buses, from BSA in 1960.

In doing so, it not only acquired a new factory but also bought a large slice of motoring history. Daimler is the oldest British motor manufacturer, the company having been formed 10 years before Rolls-Royce. Its origins lie in a chance meeting between Frederick Simms and Gottlieb Daimler at an exhibition in Bremen in 1886. Daimler built his first motor car in that year and Simms was intrigued by the idea of an internal combustion engine small enough to be mobile. He bought the patent rights to Daimler's engine for the British Empire and formed the Daimler Motor Syndicate in 1893.

Simms adopted the Daimler name for his own company out of respect for the pioneering work done by Gottlieb Daimler and he began to sell the engines for marine use. In 1896, however, he sold the Daimler rights to a professional floater of companies called Harry Lawson, who was attempting to gain a monopoly of British-held patents relating to motor manufacture. Lawson paid £35,000 for the patents and formed the Daimler Motor Company in 1896. The first British Daimler motor car was built in 1897 in Coventry. The first car owned by British royalty was a Daimler purchased by the Prince of Wales (later King Edward VII) in 1900. It was followed into the Royal Mews by a long line of further Daimlers, a fact that added to the prestige of the marque.

The company was purchased in 1910 by the Birmingham Small Arms Company, (BSA) which had been formed from an association of small armaments manufacturers in 1861. Daimler subsequently played its part in two world wars and developed a reputation for building luxurious motor cars. Even so, by the 1950s it was still not a particularly well-known marque and this was noted by Lady Docker, the new wife of BSA chairman, Sir Bernard Docker. She conceived the idea of special cars to attract publicity at the British Motor Show. The first of these appeared in 1951. It had gold plated fittings instead of the more usual chrome, and was denounced by many as too ostentatious.

By this time, however, Daimler was in decline, and had become a cause for concern at BSA. When he heard that the company might be sold, Lyons moved in. He paid £3 million. For that, Jaguar got a 56-acre site at Radford (close to its own plant at Browns Lane) and covered space of around 1 million square feet. At a stroke, Lyons had effectively doubled his factory floorspace. This was a huge step forward, without which Jaguar could probably not have made the progress it has in recent years. Daimler cars remained in production for some years, but the last true Daimler models were phased out in 1968. From then on, apart from the limousine, Daimlers were Jaguars with different radiator grilles and different badges.

Just over a year after buying Daimler, Jaguar expanded again. In October 1961, it bought Guy Motors for £800,000. Guy was a

Wolverhampton-based truck manufacturer that was in receivership. Lyons wrote in the 1961 annual report that the decision to purchase Guy flowed from the desire to move into the commercial vehicle field "as a natural addition to that of passenger vehicles". This was a reference to the Daimler Fleetline bus. In the 1960s, the truck and bus business was in general highly profitable, so the acquisition was not without its logic.

The next acquisition was Coventry Climax Engines in March 1963 through an exchange of shares. Climax manufactured forklift trucks and fire pump engines and had gained world-wide recognition through its motor racing programme. Climax engines had powered the Cooper racing cars that won the motor racing Constructors' Championship in 1959 and 1960. Lotus cars with Climax engines won the same championship in 1963 and 1965. Leonard Lee, who owned Climax, was an admirer of Lyons and welcomed an association with such a successful international company as Jaguar. For Lyons, the attraction seems to have been twofold. Climax was profitable, but the company also had a strong engineering team, including Walter Hassan, who had helped develop Jaguar's XK engine before leaving Browns Lane in 1950. Lyons wanted a new engine, preferably a 12 cylinder unit, and the existence of this team was undoubtedly persuasive in his decision to go for Coventry Climax.

Soon after this, Jaguar took over Henry Meadows, of Wolverhampton, which built marine engines and gearboxes, as well as diesel power units for trucks and railway engines. The motivation behind the takeover appears to have been that Meadows would be able to build American-designed Cummins diesel engines. The intention was that these would be fitted to Guy trucks and a planned Daimler single-deck bus. In the event, the Cummins engines were found to be unsuitable for either the truck or the bus, so the plan to build them was dropped.

But while Lyons was expanding his empire, his first love remained with Jaguar Cars, and where it was concerned, he appeared to have lost nothing of his old sureness of touch. He again rocked the motoring world in 1961 when he announced the E-Type sports car, which was closely followed by the Mark X saloon. Five years later, Lyons, who had by now been knighted, agreed to a merger with the British Motor Corporation.

By this time he was in his mid-60s, and he was increasingly concerned about Jaguar's future. He knew that it was time for him to retire, yet he had no obvious heir. His only son had been killed in a car accident in 1955. His fellow directors were, like himself, approaching retirement. The question of who would take over the running of the company was becoming pressing. Lyons's management style had caught up with him. Chairmen of other car companies had groomed their successors, but he had ignored the question.

This was not the only worry. Ever since the company had been formed, it had managed to produce a succession of remarkable cars with little research and development. However, as cars became more sophisticated and complex, and as the volume of legislation governing their design increased, development costs rose at an alarming rate. In 1967, Jaguar spent £250,000 on engineering changes to the E-type to comply with American safety and exhaust emission requirements. This was at a time when the average wage was a little more than £1,000 a year and the company was making a profit, after tax, of just over £1 million. Although Jaguar was successful, it was small by motor industry standards, and it was becoming more difficult to earn the level of profits needed to fund new model development. Any car company that cannot introduce a steady stream of new models will inevitably fail; in the specialist market in which Jaguar competes, this is especially the case. Lyons was later to deny that this question coloured his thinking in the run-up to the BMC merger. But it must have been obvious to him that Jaguar would have to find more money for research and development. Certainly, several of his directors saw this as a potential problem.

Just as important, BMC acquired Pressed Steel in 1965. BMC had been formed in 1952 from the merger of Austin, with its main factory at Longbridge, on the outskirts of Birmingham, and the Oxford-based Morris Motors. Pressed Steel had links with Morris that went back to the 1920s. William Morris, the founder of Morris Motors, saw the advantages of building car bodies from steel pressings rather than by the traditional method of fixing metal panels to a timber framework. The system had been pioneered by the Budd Manufacturing Company of Philadelphia and in the 1920s Morris encouraged the setting up of a new company, Pressed Steel, alongside his factory in Oxford to use the Budd methods under licence.

By the 1960s, all Jaguar bodies were made by Pressed Steel and, although assurances were given to Parliament that Pressed Steel would continue to serve motor industry customers outside the BMC group, Jaguar's future suddenly seemed less certain. If Pressed Steel were ever to become difficult over supplies, Jaguar could be forced out of business. Standard Triumph had faced such a threat in 1953, when BMC had acquired Fisher and Ludlow. BMC boss Leonard Lord refused to provide bodies for the new compact car that Standard Triumph needed, so the Triumph Herald had to be manufactured from small panels assembled by Standard Triumph itself. Jowett, a Yorkshire-based manufacturer that had built a reputation for producing technologically advanced cars, went out of business in 1954 after its body supplier, Briggs Bodies, was bought by Ford.

In addition, takeover fever was rife in the mid-1960s, and Lyons must have been aware that Jaguar was a prime target. It was true that he held 54 per cent of the voting shares and so could retain control of the company. Nevertheless, if someone else bought the other 46 per cent, life could be made extremely uncomfortable for him. There had, indeed, already been approaches from other manufacturers, attracted not only by Jaguar's profit potential, but also by the idea of creating a larger manufacturing company. The men who ran the British motor industry were becoming increasingly concerned that the relatively small size of their companies put them at a disadvantage compared with manufacturers in Europe and America.

At the first post-war British Motor Show, in 1948, there had been 31 British-based manufacturers. Within 20 years, mergers, takeovers and failures had reduced the number to 10, although several still produced cars under various names. Of those that remained, Ford was an offshoot of Ford of America and Vauxhall was owned by General Motors. In 1964, Chrysler took a control-ling interest in the Rootes Group; that left Jaguar, Rover, BMC and Leyland – which owned Standard Triumph – as the only major British-owned companies. In the same year, BMC and Leyland Motors began negotiations on what was seen by BMC as the takeover of Leyland. The talks failed, however, largely because of the different ways in which the shares of the two companies were seen by the stock market. Leyland was growth stock with a high share price and low yield. BMC, on the other hand, was seen as income stock with a high yield.

Leyland now turned its attention to Rover, which it bought in 1966. This development worried Jaguar. Many of the company's dealers also sold Rovers and Jaguar's UK sales manager, feared that Leyland would put pressure on them to sell only Rover and Standard-Triumph products. It so happened that Jaguar was going through a difficult period. The original Mark X, a very large, luxury saloon, was proving less successful than had been hoped, and the middle-range S-Type saloon was, in one manager's words, ". . . a very difficult car to sell". Had Leyland put pressure on the dealers then, they would probably have dropped Jaguar. According to John Morgan, now Jaguar's head of European sales, Lyons was looking for a way of protecting UK sales in the event of his dealers giving up the Jaguar franchise. At a meeting with BMC managing director Joe Edwards in Lyons's office, over the Jaguar showroom in Piccadilly, Lyons broached the idea of a merger. "He said we had the whole of the body capacity which was his lifeblood," Edwards recalls. Edwards discussed the matter with BMC chairman Sir George Harriman. "On the basis of that, we talked to Bill and we did a deal." Edwards and Harriman were attracted to Jaguar partly because of the profits it generated, but also because BMC was going through a difficult sales period. They felt that adding the Jaguar name to BMC would help restore the company's fortunes.

They also recognised that the addition of the Jaguar and Daimler ranges would relieve them of the problems of making luxury saloons and large sports cars. Ron Lucas, who was BMC finance director, explains that the merger enabled BMC to scrap the unsuccessful Princess 4 litre R. BMC was also developing a new sports car, known as the big Healey. "It may or may not have been any good, but it never went into production because the arrival of Jaguar meant that we didn't have to bother with it," Lucas says. The proposal was that BMC would acquire Jaguar but Lyons would continue to run it. "We knew that Bill was a martinet," Edwards says. "But we knew that he ran his outfit very well. The last thing we wanted to do was to ruffle Bill's feathers and why should we? He was a highly successful man, well respected in the industry, so we played him with kid gloves." That suited Lyons well, and negotiations went ahead for what was seen at BMC as a takeover and at Jaguar as a merger. All the talking was done by Lyons and Harriman. Lucas knew little about what progress was being made until one afternoon, Harriman looked into his office and said they should go to see Lyons to persuade him to come to an agreement.

Harriman was worried that word about the negotiations would leak out, so they took the Austin 1100 that he used in the factory. When they approached Browns Lane, Lucas recalls Harriman put on a pair of dark glasses and a hat. The Jaguar security guard asked them if they had an appointment. "Yes," said Harriman, "it's Lucas." "He didn't say that it was Joseph Lucas," [the electrical components supplier] Lucas says, "but he gave that impression." The two men spent some time talking to Lyons, but failed to come to an agreement. "There was a substantial amount of loan stock issued within Jaguar," Lucas recalls. "The disposition of this was one of the things worrying Bill Lyons." A few days later, Harriman and Lucas went to Lyons's home, Wappenbury Hall, to carry on the discussions. When they arrived, they found the Jaguar chief in his imposing entrance hall, with golf clubs and suitcases on the floor. Harriman asked what he was doing, and Lyons explained that he was calculating the minimum requirements for the boot space of a new car.

The three men agreed on a deal that could be recommended to the shareholders of Jaguar and BMC. But first, the details had to be agreed by the two boards. Typically, Lyons adopted a ploy to avoid giving the impression of dictating to his directors. Lucas, who had gone to Scotland on holiday immediately after the meeting with Lyons, returned to his hotel one day to find a message asking him to telephone Harriman urgently. Harriman asked him to return at once to talk to the Jaguar board. He said the Jaguar directors would not agree to the merger. "I said that was codswallop," Lucas recalls. "Everyone knew the board did what Lyons told them." Harriman was adamant, however, so Lucas went to Browns Lane and persuaded the Jaguar board to accept the deal. "Lyons wouldn't be seen to belabour his board into agreement," Lucas says. "He'd let somebody else do it."

The proposal was announced on July 11, 1966. A new company called British Motor Holdings was to be formed, made up of Jaguar, BMC and Pressed Steel. Jaguar's shareholders were offered a mixture of BMC shares and loan stock equivalent to 50s 3d for each Jaguar Ordinary share and 38s for each Jaguar "A" share, well above the market prices of the stock. The value of the deal was about £18.3 million. On August 30, BMC announced that the offer was unconditional, and by September 14 it had been accepted by the holders of more than 90 per cent of each class of Jaguar share. The merger was accomplished. Harriman was to be chairman of the new company; Lyons would be a director, while continuing as chairman of Jaguar.

The statement issued said that the merger was "in line with the world trend towards larger and more comprehensive units possessing the greatest possible resources for the development, manufacturing and marketing of a complete range of products". It pointed out the economies of scale that could be achieved by the new group and added that the two product ranges were "complementary rather than competitive". The merger did indeed have a great deal of logic behind it. Although the new group would be building a total of nine marques, Jaguar products faced no competition from BMC.

One line in the statement might have triggered concern among Jaguar enthusiasts: "We both share the opinion that if the British motor industry is to remain competitive, a closer integration of the various units must be achieved." Could it be that the words, "closer integration" were a signal that Jaguar's identity would be eroded? Daimler had all but died as a separate marque; could Jaguar go the same way? No one could tell. Attempts were made to allay these fears with statements to the press about Jaguar retaining "the greatest possible degree of autonomy" and, for two years, it looked as if that would indeed by the case.

BMH was to be too short-lived, however, for much progress to be made in bringing Jaguar and BMC together. There were discussions about common buying of some components, although BMC managers soon discovered that the size of orders was not always the only factor that determined price. Jaguar, under the influence of deputy chairman Arthur Whittaker, had driven some hard bargains and BMC found, to its surprise, that Jaguar had been able to buy some components more cheaply than BMC because manufacturers wanted the kudos of supplying Jaguar.

The most important decision affected the United States. Lyons agreed that BMC would take over responsibility for US sales. This came as a shock to John Morgan, who had taken over responsibility for export sales. "We had beautiful premises in East 57th street," he says, "lovely panelled showrooms . . . very suitable for Jaguar." Within a short time, these showrooms were vacated and operations moved to the BMC offices in New Jersey. Given that Lyons succeeded in retaining control of all the other Jaguar operations, it seems odd that he relinquished North America. Morgan never found out why it happened, though he believes Lyons was still under the impression that the coupling of BMC and Jaguar would be a merger in the true sense of the word, with equal rights for both partners. Morgan points out that Lyons was always suspicious of America as a market because of its volatility. (Between 1966 and 1971, US sales accounted for anything between 17 per cent and 30 per cent of the total.) "He (Lyons) had two or three shocks in the early days, when he had produced cars for the States and then they had called off and not taken them," explains Morgan. "He had a terrible fear of being landed wih lots of American specification cars, so I think he was glad to hand it over because he had complete faith in George Harriman."

That, however, appears to have been the most important

instance of a joint approach. There was a joint management board, which consisted of the directors of Jaguar and the executive directors of BMC. Lucas comments: "I don't think we ever did anything, but we used to meet once a month to draw the demarcation lines between the two organisations." Although the attempted merger between BMC and Leyland had fallen through, many still hoped that the two companies could co-operate. Among them was Tony Benn, Minister of Technology. There was no doubt in government circles that the British motor industry was heading for trouble. The Department of Economic Affairs predicted that the motor industry would be "one of the problem areas of the 1970s".

There was more than a touch of irony in this, since at least some of the manufacturers' problems stemmed from economic measures introduced by successive governments. Throughout the 1960s and 1970s, hire purchase restrictions were varied to regulate consumer demand. In 1960, car buyers had to pay a 20 per cent minimum deposit and the balance over 24 months. A few months later, the repayment period was extended to 36 months. The most stringent restrictions were applied in 1966, when car buyers had to pay a 40 per cent deposit and could spread the balance over 24 months. Between the beginning of 1965 and the end of 1967, there were no less than seven major changes in hire purchase regulations. At the same time, excise duty was increased from 14 pence a gallon in 1961 to 22.5 pence a gallon in 1969. Purchase tax, which stood at 55 per cent in 1961, fell by stages to 27.5 per cent in 1966 before rising again to 36.66 per cent in 1968. Unpredictable variations in demand were the result.

In December 1966, the Labour government of Harold Wilson created the Industrial Reorganisation Corporation, with the intention of accelerating change in British industry. The IRC began to encourage greater co-operation between Leyland and BMH early in 1967. Discussions between the two companies dragged on through the summer. The difficulties revolved around money and people. On the financial side, BMH's profit forecasts occupied many hours of discussion. Even so, it was to prove far more difficult to satisfy the people concerned in the merger. There were three key characters: Harriman, Edwards and Leyland chairman Sir Donald Stokes. (Lyons stayed on the sidelines.)

Some years previously, Joe Edwards had been director of manufacture at BMC, and he and Harriman were the two candidates to succeed Leonard Lord as chairman. Lord decided that Harriman was right for the job, and to avoid the appearance of uncertainty with two "crown princes", he sacked Edwards in 1956. Edwards went to Pressed Steel, and Harriman duly took over from Lord in 1961. After the takeover of Pressed Steel by BMC, Edwards was made managing director of BMC in June, 1966, under Harriman. Now, Harriman was clearly destined to be chairman of the group that would be formed by the merger of BMH and Leyland. That left Stokes and Edwards, and neither was prepared to defer to the other. Edwards did not learn of the talks with Leyland until after he had moved back into BMC. "Suddenly, George told me he was having talks with Donald," he says. "I thought, it's the same thing all over again." He made his position abundantly clear to the BMH board. "I told them, I want you to know that if this thing goes through you can count me out."

Edwards saw Stokes as being in the same mould as Lord, which is, perhaps, misjudging Stokes. Lord is often described as vindictive, dictatorial and bullying, and although Stokes's reputation might have invited such a comparison, he was actually much less of a strong man than was often claimed. Nevertheless, Edwards had formed a view of Stokes and foresaw problems. Perhaps most important, however, was his seniority. "I wasn't going to work for Stokes," he says now. "Why should I? I was managing director of a much bigger outfit than his." One of the solutions proposed by Harriman was that Edwards and Stokes would be executive vice chairmen. Edwards would be in charge of production and Stokes in charge of sales. Stokes, however, was not prepared to be joint number two and Edwards steadfastly refused to work for Stokes.

In December, Harriman suggested that, if the two companies were to merge, BMC, Jaguar and Pressed Steel should continue to operate as autonomous units. Stokes, however, insisted that there should be a single corporation, not a loose amalgamation of separate companies. Yet Stokes' actions at Leyland after acquiring Standard-Triumph and Rover belied his firmness. Malcolm Hart, who then worked at Standard-Triumph's London sales office, recalls Stokes telling dealers that the two companies would work together but would remain as separate entities. Geoffrey Robinson, who was to join the British Leyland Motor Corporation from the IRC, also casts doubt on Stokes's intentions. "I don't think he had a clear idea of what he wanted to do with the company," he says.

The talks had reached an impasse, and Benn suggested a mediator in the shape of Sir Frank Kearton, chairman of the IRC and of Courtaulds. His task was not easy, for Stokes was beginning to lose patience. He pondered a takeover bid; the idea was resisted by, among others Prime Minister Wilson. BMH would certainly have fought such a bid, and the confrontation would have damaged both companies.

On January 15, 1968, the personality problem finally seemed to have been solved when Edwards gave way to the inevitable and agreed to work for Stokes. He felt he had been pushed into a corner where he had only two options – to accept Stokes as his boss or to get out. This had been the most intractable problem, and it seems surprising in retrospect that the merger was held up for so long over the position of one man. But Harriman was loyal to his managing director throughout. The next day, a document detailing the merger agreement and the future management structure was signed by the directors of both companies. On February 8, the British Leyland Motor Corporation was incorporated as a private company. This was the first step towards acquiring all the interests of BMH and Leyland. For Lyons and Jaguar, the agreement document was bad news. It stated that the subsidiary companies would become divisions of the new corporation.

Lyons, however, was not one to give up so easily. The new corporation was still not a reality, but a "dummy" board meeting was held in order to ensure that all the participants would know what was going on. Lyons took the opportunity to raise the question of his personal control, a matter that he had aired several times during the negotiations. He agreed to co-operate as fully as possible, but he said he expected to run his company as he had always done, without reference to anyone else. The meeting had already been very acrimonious, with Edwards giving full vent to his feelings towards Stokes. In conceding autonomy for Jaguar, Stokes probably felt that he had enough trouble on his hands already without starting an argument with Lyons. Today, he insists that he was motivated purely by respect for Lyons: "Bill Lyons was a man of some stature in the industry and I was happy to have him as deputy chairman and to let him go on running Jaguar." Perhaps the reason was merely that Lyons had the stronger character. Whatever it was Stokes stated that he did not intend to interfere at Jaguar. That conflicted with the policy agreed and signed less than a month previously.

Lyons, however, was about to become more deeply embroiled in the formation of the new company as a result of a conversation between Lucas and a group of Leyland directors. After the dummy board meeting Lucas had drinks with some of the Leyland directors and two of the BMH directors. "In the course of the hour or so, Jack Plane and Bertie Fogg (Leyland directors) did a bit of pumping around the place," Lucas says. "I got a bit cross about all this and I got sarcastic. That's a great mistake, because if you're sarcastic and it's subsequently written down, it doesn't appear to be sarcastic."

The critical moment came when Stokes said that he thought BMH was not very healthy financially. Lucas relates: "I said, oh yes, of course, we're just about to go broke." He uttered the words with what was intended to be an air of heavy sarcasm, but they were pounced on by the Leyland Directors. Unfortunately, BMH's figures for the first half of the year had not been good; a profit of around £1 million was expected. The forecast for the full year had been around £16 million. Lucas claims that, had a previous method of calculating depreciation been retained, his profit forecast for the year would not have been far wrong.

The first-half results had been affected by a strike at BMC. External factors had included a credit squeeze, a rise of 2 per cent in the bank rate and a 14 per cent rise in the price of petrol, all of which accompanied the devaluation of the pound in November

1967. All this was bound to affect the sales performance and profit of the group. The previous November, A. L. Kingshott, Ford of Britain's treasurer, had been quoted as saying that the British motor industry as a whole would lose £32 million during the next year.

Stokes told the IRC that he would have to call the merger off. The information that he had planned to give to his shareholders now appeared to be inaccurate. Rather than allow the deal to be aborted, Kearton said the IRC would support a bid by Leyland for BMH. The BMH board, however, did not want a takeover; it wanted a merger on equal terms. So Kearton suggested that, if the merger went ahead, Harriman should retire as chairman of the new corporation. In his book *The Leyland Papers*, Graham Turner claims that Lyons was one of the men suggested as his successor. Edwards, along with many others, denies any knowledge of such a suggestion. "I don't think he would have been right for it and I don't think he would have wanted it," he says. Whether or not Turner's claim is true, Kearton then proposed that Stokes should become chairman.

The BMH board discussed the proposal and Lyons suggested that he should talk to Stokes. He had, by this time, become a pivotal figure. He knew and liked Harriman, was friendly with Edwards, had a good relationship with Kearton and had won the respect of Stokes. He took on the task of trying to save Harriman's job. There was never any chance of achieving this, however. Leyland was demanding that Harriman should resign as chairman, although it was prepared to let him stay on the board. That was its price for keeping to the merger deal. If Harriman refused to go, Leyland would launch a takeover bid. BMH was in no position to fight this with any hope of success. Harriman asked each of the BMH directors if they thought the merger should go ahead. With the exception of Edwards, they all agreed that it should. Harriman was left with no alternative but to say that he would resign.

It was then pointed out that Harriman was president of the Society of Motor Manufacturers and Traders. He could not retain that position if he was no longer with a manufacturer, so it was agreed that he would remain as chairman until his term expired in November 1968. As work began on letters confirming the arrangement, Harriman suffered a severe nose bleed. A doctor found that his pulse was low and his blood pressure alarmingly high. He was taken to a clinic and told to rest for two weeks. However, the Leyland annual general meeting was due to take place in two days' time, on February 20, and Harriman had to sign his letter before the shareholders gathered. It was taken to him in the London Clinic where he signed it. He announced his retirement in September. Edwards, having decided that he could not work with Stokes after all, had left five months earlier.

The British Leyland Motor Corporation was now a reality with Stokes at its head. The aim had been to create a British motor manufacturer that was big enough to compete with those in the rest of Europe and in America. Lyons supported the merger because he felt that a closer commercial relationship between British manufacturers was needed, particularly in export markets. In terms of size, BLMC was second only to Volkswagen outside the US. But it had emerged so quickly that Jaguar was now a part of an organisation that had still not recovered from the effects of previous mergers.

In 1960, Jaguar had acquired Daimler and followed that by buying Guy in 1961. The same year, Standard-Triumph had been taken into the Leyland fold. In 1963, Jaguar had bought Coventry Climax and added Henry Meadows to its empire a year later. The merger between BMC and Jaguar had taken place in 1966 with Rover joining Leyland in 1967. The whole forest of companies was then, theoretically, brought together in 1968 by the formation of BLMC. Within the space of eight years, there had been nine mergers, takeovers or acquisitions. The effect of this at Jaguar was to spread management talent even more thinly.

The company had always been run on the basis of the minimum number of people necessary to do the job. As new companies joined what was becoming the Jaguar group, managers found that they had to cope with an additional workload. Lyons preferred to work with people he knew. For example, when it became necessary to launch a new bus after the purchase of Daimler, it was Jaguar people who had to do it. The fact that they were so successful reflects great credit on them. The Daimler Fleetline bus, for example, became a best seller. Guy's Big J trucks were similarly successful, but the effort involved in these new activities meant managers could devote less attention to Jaguar cars.

However, the intractable difficulties at Austin Morris meant that Lyons was left to look after Jaguar with little interference. "We had much more serious problems than worrying about Jaguar," Stokes says. "Bill Lyons was left to run that."

Unfortunately, the new management appeared not to understand the people working within BMH. By the first BLMC annual meeting, in February 1969, only three of the 10 directors had been in the BMH organisation. In fact, the Leyland people were aggravating an already difficult situation. The two organisations that had been brought together to form BMC had been fighting between themselves for years. Now, it became a multi-faceted battle. Each of the individual companies continued to operate separately, with individual accounts for each. Sales executive Hart recalls that there was no communication between the different organisations. Stokes insists that immediate integration was out of the question. "We had a tremendous business to digest," he says. "There was all sorts of overlapping, supplies going all over the country and criss-crossing. We were trying to eliminate all that and you could only move at a certain pace. We wanted to try to take people with us."

Nor was there any attempt to rush through integration of the dealer networks. Part of the reason for this was the strength of the dealer councils. These bodies represented the interests of the dealers to BLMC, and they were not about to agree to a programme of integration that would see some of their number losing their franchises. Even so, after a year or two, informal discussions began to take place about dealers. At this time, there were several separate dealer networks – Austin, Morris, Rover, Standard-Triumph and Jaguar. "It was pretty clear that the Standard-Triumph network was not very good," Hart says. "Since there were a number of common BMC and Standard-Triumph dealers, we started informal discussions in the late 1960s about which dealers we saw as being stable in the long term. But it was not a structured franchising meeting. It was just a series of ad hoc discussions."

Hart recalls that Jaguar stood apart, even from such informal links. "They were really autonomous in those days. The prospect of linking the Jaguar franchise to anyone else's or even discussing dealers was pretty remote." It is true that Jaguar shared some dealers with Rover, but there was a big difference between freely choosing a dealer who might also handle Rover, and having to give a Jaguar franchise to a Rover dealer.

On the manufacturing side, BLMC included many well known names such as Austin, Austin Healey, Daimler, Jaguar, MG, Morris, Riley, Rover, Triumph, Vanden Plas and Wolseley. At the time, *Autocar* magazine listed no less than 40 different models from BLMC's car-making divisions, although when allowance was made for the company's version of badge engineering, that figure was reduced to 23 body shapes and 16 engines. BLMC was often criticised for producing the same car with different badges. In fact, it did not even do that very well. The Mini, for example, was produced as both an Austin and a Morris, but the other two badge derivatives, the Riley Elf and the Wolseley Hornet, had different bonnets and boots, thus removing some of the cost advantages of true badge engineering.

All of these cars were effectively built by three separate divisions. Austin and Morris were the volume manufacturers, building cars such as the Mini, the 1100 and 1300 range, the 1800, the MG Midget and MGB. Rover-Triumph filled the middle ground with cars such as the Triumph Herald, the Rover 2000, the Rover 3.5 litre, the Triumph Spitfire, and the Triumph 2000. Jaguar was in the luxury sector.

If the idea that had brought the group into being had been carried through, the unwieldy and complex model range would have been drastically reduced. This could have brought cost savings by reducing the number of different bodies, engines and transmissions. Inevitably, many historic and much loved marque names would have disappeared as a result. But the new management found the complexities of its hard-won empire far beyond anything it had expected. Limited management resources were fully occupied trying to sort out the mess. So BLMC continued to operate as a loose amalgamation of fiercely independent companies.

Even so, something had to be done about the dealer networks. The choice was either drastically to reduce the networks or to allow them to carry on existing side by side. Within the company, it was suggested that there should be two dealer bodies. One would sell Austin and Morris cars while the other sold Jaguar, Rover, Triumph, MG and any other marque that could be termed specialist, rather than volume. This would have created one network that was cohesive and one that was a rag bag. Alternatively, one dealer organisation would sell Morris, MG and Jaguar, while the other would sell Austin, Rover and Triumph. Neither option was welcome at Jaguar.

Another faction suggested that there should be three dealer organisations, one for Austin, one for Morris and a third for Jaguar, Rover and Triumph. This was the approach favoured by Stokes and, as the boss, he had the final word. The legacy of this decision was still being felt in the 1980s. By that time, sales had fallen to the point where the number of dealers had to be reduced in order to provide viable businesses for those that remained.

The sales arrangements overseas were often even more complicated, but here, BLMC faced up to the difficulties, although the results were far from acceptable to Jaguar. The first market to be tackled was South Africa. The Austin and Morris networks were combined and then given Jaguar, Rover and Triumph franchises. This meant that some Jaguar dealers were fired. In Australia, all Jaguar's distributors went and the franchise was given to the Leyland Motor Corporation of Australia, largely because that company was losing money and needed the profits that were theoretically available from Jaguar sales.

Jaguar (France) came in for similar treatment. John Morgan, who ran it for a time, explains: "We sold 1,000 cars in 10 months and made £320,000 profit." Up to that point, he says, BLMC had shown little interest in the operation. "Then they suddenly realised that Aveling Barford [BLMC's construction machinery division] was losing half a million pounds that year in France. So we were quickly merged to offset the losses at Aveling Barford and we were distributed by Aveling Barford." Within a short time, Austin Morris dealers throughout France were given the Jaguar franchise. In Denmark, too, the Austin distributor was given Jaguar along with Triumph. This was seen by Jaguar as a massacre of its dealer network, particularly in Europe. As one manager put it: "Jaguar became merely a product in the European markets. It had no special identity. It had no special characteristics. It was treated as just another car."

According to Stokes, this approach enabled BLMC to reap the profits that had previously flowed to foreign importers: "Overseas, the real profit lies in being an importer. So we became an importer in Spain and in France and Holland and all these other countries. We creamed off the profit which previously, the importers had been getting rich on." Morgan sees it differently, however. "They never made any money as importers in export markets. That was their problem. They lost money in every market where they had an import company, as far as I am aware." He says that indemnity payments made to compensate dealers in Europe who were losing their franchises were then used by those dealers to take on Japanese franchises. "That was the demise of British cars in Europe."

At the same time, attempts were made to simplify BLMC's range. Rover had been developing a new, large saloon for some years. Code named P8, it was intended to be luxurious, fast and very well equipped, and its designers were confident that it would take sales from Jaguar's large saloons. That made commercial sense when Jaguar and Rover were rivals, but once they were owned by the same company, such competition would damage the group as a whole. Added to that, BLMC had limited engineering and cash resources for the development of new products. Stokes took the view that these resources should be devoted to developing new volume cars, since very little was under development at Austin Morris. So P8 was cancelled in 1971, 12 months before it was due to be launched, after about £5 million had been spent on it.

The same fate befell another Rover project: the P6BS two-seater sports car. This was, by all accounts, an outstanding vehicle. But apart from the lack of engineers and money to develop it, Stokes was unsure of the the car's potential. "Although it was a beautiful car, we weren't sure whether there was a market for it." The P6BS would also have competed with Jaguar's E-Type. This project was cancelled in 1969. At Rover, it was felt that Lyons had a hand in these decisions and, as BLMC deputy chairman, he was certainly in a powerful position to put Jaguar's case. Stokes, however, denies that there was any pressure from Lyons: "He wasn't like that. He didn't try to stop them. He was a very objective man, and took an overall view." Nevertheless, the antagonism that the belief created was typical of the inter-company rivalries, often bordering on open hostility, that lay on the path to creating a cohesive corporation.

There was an attempt to use Lyons's styling skills in other parts of the corporation. Stokes recalls Lyons going to Austin-Morris styling meetings and giving his advice. "But his heart wasn't in it, his heart was in Jaguar. That was what he was interested in."

While future product plans were being sorted out, Jaguar and Rover-Triumph were notionally brought together as "specialist cars". Bob Berry, the former Jaguar PR manager, was moved to Leyland International to oversee its marketing. He recalls a unit being set up with around half a dozen people in it. "It was allowed to express the need for specialisation within BLMC," he explains. "I think it only acted as a touch on the rudder, but it was able, to some extent, to give greater identity to the marketing of specialist cars, particularly in Europe. But it was a very half-hearted attempt by BLMC to recognise the particular needs of specialist cars." The unit's efforts were small compared with the attention given to volume cars.

Geoffrey Robinson, who was to become chief executive at Jaguar, claims that the existence of the international division was a major difficulty for Jaguar. According to him, the company had direct control only over UK sales; the international division could choose its own route in selling Jaguars abroad. At factory level, the grouping of specialist cars meant little, since managers still operated as if their companies were independent. David Andrews, who was to become executive vice chairman of BL recalls that

Jaguar, Rover and Triumph in particular, tended to compete among themselves rather than with outsiders. "They seemed to be oblivious to what was happening on the continent," he says. "None of them seemed to have the slightest idea of the scale of Mercedes-Benz business, for example. I found it astonishing. It wasn't taken into account as a competitive situation."

BLMC was never able to overcome the independent attitudes of each company management and, at an operational level, it does not appear to have tried very hard. Changes such as the merging of Rover and Triumph served only to make the employees of each of the companies unsure of their positions. The effect of such uncertainty at Jaguar was disastrous. Everyone who worked for the company felt an intense loyalty to it. They worked for Jaguar, not British Leyland, and they were proud of it. As the impact of BLMC on Jaguar was increasingly felt, employees at every level began to close ranks. They resented the outsiders who, they felt, did not understand the company and its traditions.

Sir William Lyons retired as chairman in 1972, aged 70, although he remained as president, and F. R. W. (Lofty) England took over as chairman and chief executive. England had started his working life as an apprentice at the London Daimler works in 1927. Between finishing his apprenticeship and World War II, he was both a racing mechanic and a racing driver between spells working for Alvis. In 1941, he volunteered for the RAF and became a Lancaster bomber pilot. After the war he returned to Alvis in Coventry and it was from there that he was recruited to become Jaguar service manager in 1946.

His racing experience was put to good use when he added the job of racing manager to that of Service Manager in the early 1950s. Under England's leadership, Jaguar won the Le Mans 24 hour race in 1951 and 1953 with the C-Type racing car and in 1955, with the D-Type. Both cars had been designed for the job of winning at Le Mans and they did it convincingly. But Jaguar had withdrawn from official participation in racing by the time England was appointed assistant managing director in 1961. He was subsequently appointed joint managing director in 1968. Almost everyone who came into contact with England liked him and is reluctant to criticise him, but no one believes he was the right man to take on the chairmanship. As one former colleague put it: "Lofty was a great engineer. If he could have run the company as well as he could fix an engine, things would have been much better." But Lyons wanted England to succeed him, and the BLMC management accepted his recommendation.

Soon after England took over, Jaguar was hit by a damaging strike over the change from piecework to measured day work. Traditionally, the industry had paid its assembly workers according to the amount of work done during a shift. The new method of payment involved assessing the amount of work that one person could complete in a shift and paying a flat rate based on that calculation. The unions objected to the change. The strike was the longest strike in the company's history; it dragged on for 10 weeks before being resolved. Once it was over, England was able to address himself to the question of his successor. That might seem premature, but England was 60 years old and felt that whoever took over from him should have time to work his way into the job before being left to get on with it.

BLMC management appears to have taken the view that, now Lyons had retired, it was time to take a firm grip on Jaguar. Stokes telephoned England in September 1973 and suggested that Geoffrey Robinson should be brought in as managing director. Robinson was only 34 years old at the time and had been running Innocenti, British Leyland's Italian subsidiary, for 16 months. He had a BA in Russian and German from Cambridge, and an Economics MA from Yale. He had joined BLMC from the Industrial Reorganisation Corporation and had been made financial controller for the whole group at the age of 30. His appointment as managing director of Jaguar was announced on September 7, 1973.

He began to make his mark almost immediately, in a way that must have startled England, who had envisaged a prolonged period of "grooming" for his successor. Robinson's view was quite different, judging from his comments in the press. He saw himself running the company with advice from England. Robinson was close to John Barber, who was now managing director of BLMC, and who is said to have been the moving force behind the attempts to form BLMC into a cohesive corporation, in the image of Ford. The managers of the various divisions were not interested in Barber's approach. Robinson recalls attempts to introduce corporate controls on Jaguar. "I said, look John, I want to be responsible. If it goes well, I'll hopefully get the credit. If it goes badly, kick me out, but I don't want to be second guessed by your corporate staffs." Robinson's view was that the company could never be run in the way that Ford operated. Ford managers had grown up with centralised control. In BLMC, there were so many disparate parts to the organisation that it could never be made into a single entity.

So Robinson effectively declared independence from the beginning, and began to tackle what he saw as Jaguar's most pressing problems. He did not judge sales to be a problem. "I inherited a two and a half, three year order book. I thought the one thing I didn't have to worry about was sales. That was a mistake."

Robinson fell victim to the way Jaguar had done business in the past. Dealers knew they would never receive all the cars they ordered. To overcome that, they overstated their requirements. Lulled into a false sense of security, Robinson set about determining the areas that needed immediate attention. He quickly replaced the heads of production, purchasing, finance and personnel. Only the men running research and development and sales were retained.

Robinson is unrepentant about removing so many long-standing Jaguar people. "I made no prejudgements whatsoever," he says. "But I wanted improved performance right across the board. Where I thought the company was lacking in management, we changed it." Ken Edwards joined as a personnel director shortly after Robinson took up his new job. "The big problem was that there was no one left here who knew how to take decisions," he says. That, he maintains, resulted from Lyons's long years of total domination of the company. "The main thing that Geoffrey did was to change Jaguar from a company that was dominated by Sir William to a company that had a team."

The company's approach to industrial relations also changed.

Robinson spent much time building good relationships with union officials and was criticised by dealers and some managers for becoming too friendly with them. Edwards is less ready to condemn him, however. "You have to see it in the context of the whole BL scene," he explains. "The relationships with the unions in BL as a whole, were not good. I think his (Robinson's) relationships with the unions were quite reasonable."

Robinson says his first priority was to improve the quality of the cars, though few today are prepared to admit that he made any headway. One of the curiosities of the company is that, although Jaguars have always felt like quality products, with their leather and walnut interiors, quality of manufacture was not, for many years, a major concern. E-types today, for example, are much sought after, but the bodies frequently need extensive rebuilds owing to the ravages of rust. As one dealer explains: "Within two years, a Jaguar would begin to rust in those days, but it didn't matter because they represented a lot of motor car for the money."

Stokes comments: "When I went to the States or on various trips around the world, the quality reports I got on Jaguars were bad. They were very good motor cars that were spoilt by quality control problems, most of which, to be fair, were not of Jaguar's making. A lot of them were from suppliers." Robinson agrees that the company did not demand sufficiently high standards from its suppliers. "The trouble was that the Jaguar engineers were so much better than the suppliers," he says. "They were victims of their own cleverness really. Jaguar put far too much faith in its suppliers."

Ian Forster was brought in as purchasing director in 1974 and he began to impose tighter quality control procedures on the suppliers. As this was happening, Robinson announced an investment plan to increase production from 30,000 to 60,000 cars by the end of 1975. Doubling the production of a company like Jaguar in less than two years was a formidable undertaking. Selling them would have been even more difficult with the effects of the first fuel crisis already being felt in the market. The drive for increased production, however, exacerbated the quality problems.

A former Pressed Steel inspector remembers refusing to pass bodies as fit for delivery to Jaguar. He was overruled in order to maintain deliveries.

A significant part of the expansion was a new paint plant. Mike Beasley was brought in as production engineer in 1974 to oversee the planning and building of this. He spent his first few months revising existing plans for the plant, a process that he describes as normal when an important new facility is created. Robinson saw this as only the first stage of expansion. Once the paint plant was installed, he envisaged a new factory to build car bodies. At the same time, Beasley was also involved in trying to create more space in the final assembly areas of the factory, which were very cramped. During the early stages, Robinson was not even full time managing director. He was still involved with Innocenti and would often fly back to Italy on a Friday night, returning to Coventry on Sunday night or Monday morning.

Under Robinson, production rose by nearly 10 per cent, and this made considerable demands on his managers. Bob Berry, who had returned to Browns Lane, recalls many out of hours meetings, which often took place at the Post House hotel. "He was living at the Post House, and when he held meetings on a Sunday morning, which was frequently, they'd take place in his bedroom. We'd sit on the bed and on the floor with an endless supply of coffee."

Robinson's approach was too much for England, who announced his retirement from the company in January 1974. By this time, there were few "Jaguar men" left at senior management levels in the company. Nor was Robinson popular with his colleagues in the rest of BLMC. "Geoffrey made a lot of enemies because he was very outspoken," recalls Stokes. "People didn't like it when he grumbled about the quality of the bodies he was getting from Pressed Steel. He was quite right to grumble." Many of the managers who worked under Robinson, however, express admiration for his attempts to bring Jaguar up to date. Beasley recalls: "I worked for him for only six or eight months, but he was an unusual boss. I'd never had one who gave me quite so much freedom." Another former colleague says: "He gave us the job of managing our areas. That was a new experience for a lot of us."

The new managing director was promising levels of investment that could never have been achieved had Jaguar been independent, but developments elsewhere in BLMC were soon to put an end to this prospect. BLMC's profit record was fluctuating. Group pre-tax profits for 1968 had been £38 million on sales of £907 million. This rose to £40 million on turnover of £970 million in 1969 before plunging to a mere £4 million in 1970, although sales had risen to £1,021 million. 1971 saw a recovery to £32 million with sales up to £1,177 million. In 1972, turnover of £1,281 million produced profits of £32 million. The following year, 1.16 million vehicles were produced, sales reached £1,564 million, and pre-tax profits stood at £51 million.

During the summer of 1973, the company began to lay down investment plans for the next five to six years. The government was interested in these since there was a possibility that new factories could be bult in assisted areas of the country. That would have given BLMC the possibility of grants under the 1972 Industry Act. As was to be the case so often, however, the company was blown off course by outside events. The Yom Kippur War started on October 6. Eleven days later, the Arab oil producers announced a cut in supplies in an attempt to bring pressure to bear on Israel to withdraw from occupied territories. Under the impact of the oil crisis, sales of new cars in Britain plummeted. In 1974, they were more than 23 per cent down. That year, in response to a dispute in the coal industry, the British government imposed a three-day working week in an attempt to conserve fuel supplies. The resulting recession and a steadily rising rate of inflation led BLMC to revise its plans. The figures were horrifying. In the autumn of 1973, the group had expected to earn a pre-tax profit of £68 million during its 1973–74 financial year. In fact, the first six months of the year produced a loss of £16 million, and there was no prospect of improvement.

In 1972, 1.6 million cars had been sold in Britain. By 1974, this had dropped to 1.2 million. At Jaguar, the effects of the fuel crisis seem to have been weathered remarkably well. The Series 2 XJ6 and XJ12 were announced in the autumn of 1973, and the company sold 14,493 cars in the UK during 1974, a figure that had only been surpassed by the 15,416 recorded in 1971. The message of BLMC's overall financial performance, however, was clear. Capital investment had to be cut back to a minimum. Even so, the company was not making enough profit to finance it. The four clearing banks – Barclays, Lloyds, Midland and National Westminster – were approached for help. The company felt that it needed £507 million spread over six years, about a tenth of it was for expansion, the remainder divided about equally between modernising outdated factories and tooling and facilities for new models. The government was concerned about the wider industrial effects of the investment cut-back, and the company told the Department of Industry what extra development could be undertaken if another £100 million were made available in addition to the loans it was attempting to raise through the banks.

Even while these discussions were going on, the situation was deteriorating. BLMC attempted to control it with a cash conservation programme, but that was not enough. The unaudited results for the full 1973–74 financial year pointed to a net loss of £9.9 million. To that, the company had to add the cost of closing down its Australian subsidiary, which was expected to be around £11.8 million. So BLMC seemed likely to make a total loss on the year of £21.7 million. The true position turned out to be even worse: the company had lost £23.95 million. At the beginning of that financial year, net liquid assets had stood at £50.7 million. By the end, there were net liabilities of £35.2 million. Alex Park, the newly appointed finance director, told the board that the company was, effectively, broke. Stokes and Ron Lucas went to see Tony Benn, and asked if the government would guarantee further loans. Benn said he would see what he could do.

By the end of November, 1974, when there was a meeting between BLMC, the banks and the government, the company had overdraft facilities of £152 million. These were expected to be fully committed during December and a further cash outflow of £30 million was forecast for January. The report and accounts for 1974 were heavily qualified by the auditors, who pointed out that BLMC had assumed it would obtain further finance in the form of guarantees from the government for a £50 million additional overdraft. However the figures were read, the group had run out of money. The banks would not extend borrowing facilities any further. The crisis was brought to a head by a strike of 800 assembly workers late in 1974 at the Triumph factory in Coventry. They had been laid off through a strike of white-collar workers at the plant. The agreement BLMC had with the unions was that no one would be paid off if they were laid off as a result of an internal dispute. The assembly workers' strike was aimed at winning payment for the lay-off. They did not get what they wanted, because the company effectively went bankrupt under them.

In an article published in *The Motor* in December, 1974, Philip Turner, the magazine's Midland editor, commented on the fact that Stokes had flown to the Middle East the day after details of the talks with the government became known. He speculated that Stokes's purpose was to try to raise money from the oil rich Arab states. Whether or not that was true, and Stokes denies it, the group was left to rely on the government.

The ramifications of BLMC's failure were so horrific that the government immediately stepped in and put together plans for a reconstruction of the group. Ironically, it was one of its architects, Tony Benn, by now Secretary of State for Industry, who had to tell the House of Commons on December 6, 1974, that ". . . because of the company's position in the economy as a leading exporter and its importance to employment both directly and through the many firms that are dependent on it, the government are informing the company's bankers that the approval of Parliament will be sought for a guarantee of the working capital required over and above existing facilities." The government estimated that, if BLMC failed, a million people would lose their jobs. With unemployment in Britain running at 600,000 for 1974, that was too awful to contemplate. Government concern also centred on BL's contribution to the nation's balance of payments. In his book *Final Term*, Harold Wilson recalled that ". . . Leyland's direct exports from Britain in 1974 had reached almost £500 million. . . ." Had BLMC been allowed to fail, the effect on the balance of trade would have been made worse by an increase in imported vehicles which would have been needed to fill the gap. Add to those figures the loss to the Exchequer caused by the fall in tax revenue and national insurance contributions, and by the costs of unemployment benefit, and it is difficult to see what avenues were open to Wilson apart from wholesale support for the company. In some quarters, it was felt that BLMC could have been sold. From Wilson's point of view that, too, was unacceptable since any buyer would almost certainly have been a foreign owned company. Wilson felt strongly that Britain needed an indigenous motor manufacturing industry.

In his statement, Benn told the House that ". . . in response to the company's request for support for their investment programme, the government also intend to introduce longer-term arrangements, including a measure of public ownership". A high-level team, led by Sir Don Ryder, would be appointed to ". . . advise on the company's situation and prospects". According to Lucas, this announcement came as a shock to the BLMC board. "My recollection is that we were expecting further discussions," he explains. "There weren't any, but Benn stood up in the House of Commons and made his announcement without any reference to us."

Ryder was, at the time, both an industrial adviser to the government and chairman designate of the National Enterprise Board, the body that had been proposed to oversee the government's holdings in several companies, including Rolls-Royce, which had failed in 1971. In this respect, it was a holding company. The NEB was clearly seen by the government as a means of extending public ownership. It would provide investment capital for manufacturing companies, taking equity stakes in them in return. This was not seen simply as a way of bailing out companies that were in difficulty. The board was to be empowered to start new ventures, extend public ownership into profitable companies, take on an entrepreneurial role in promoting reorganisation or development of industries and be a source of management and financial advice, both for industry and government. It was under the terms of this wide-ranging brief that Ryder was appointed to investigate the affairs of BLMC.

The membership of Ryder's team was announced by Benn on December 18, when he laid before the Commons the resolution to enable the government to guarantee a further £50 million of loans from the banks. In addition to Ryder, who was chairman and chief executive of Reed International, there were to be four members of the team. Robert Clark was chairman of Hill Samuel and of the Industrial Development Advisory Board. Stanley Gillen had been with Ford from 1947 to 1969. An American, his early career had been with Ford of America, but he had been managing director and chief executive for Ford of Britain from 1965 to 1967 and then vice president, manufacturing, of Ford of Europe from 1967 to 1969. Frederick McWhirter, a partner in Peat, Marwick, Mitchell, the accountancy firm, was the third member of the team and Harry Urwin, deputy general secretary of the Transport and General Workers' Union and a member of the Industrial Development Advisory Board, completed the line-up. From Jaguar's point of view, this team had one significant defect. None had any direct experience of the luxury car business. Indeed, the only member from the automotive industry was Gillen, although Urwin had been involved with the labour side of the industry. The team was supported by various people who were seconded to it, many of them ex-Ford people.

Apart from appointing the Ryder team, the government imposed a series of other conditions in return for its guarantees. BLMC had to undertake to co-operate fully with Ryder; it had to obtain approval from the secretary of state before embarking on new capital expenditure of more than £1 million; it had to give advance notice of an intention to draw money under the guarantee; and there were to be no dividend payments without prior consultation with the secretary of state. Stokes commented that these conditions effectively meant that the government had complete control over the group's activities. This was hardly surprising. The alternative, after all, would have been to call in a receiver or a liquidator, and what control would Stokes and his board have had then?

On April 23, 1975, the group asked the Stock Exchange to suspend dealings in its shares. By now, each of the 590 million ordinary 25p shares was worth just 6.25p. Reactions at BLMC to the appointment of Ryder and his team varied. Some senior executives were very antagonistic. Lower down, the response was less harsh. Part of the antagonism stemmed from the lack of motor industry experience of most of the team members. But the way in which the investigation was conducted also brought criticism. Stokes points out that the team had very few meetings with the board. "The Ryder team almost studiously avoided any consultations with the board when they were making their report," he claims. "We gave them *carte blanche* to see what they liked. There was nothing wrong with the company in the sense of misdemeanours or anything. There were economic problems, but I think the board only met the committee for half an hour."

Lower down the company, middle managers were given their chance to tell the Ryder team what they thought was wrong. Inevitably, the opportunity was grasped by many to air grievances. Stokes comments: "Of course, if you go to a foundry in Wolverhampton and they've been deprived of funds, they will say this is an awful management. If they'd only put five million into this foundry, we could have beaten the world. The problem was that we didn't have the five million."

For sales volume and market penetration forecasts, Ryder had to rely on BLMC's own staff. Market forecasters at the company have a remarkable record of accurately forecasting future demand for new cars and the figures in the Ryder report bear this out. But difficulties arose over sales and penetration forecasts. According to one of the people responsible for compiling these figures, Ryder was fed with inflated numbers at the request of senior managers. It was an example of corporate politics at work. Within the company, several different forecasts were produced. One set would be for budgeting; another for declaration to manufacturing staff; a third for the dealer network; still another, yet more optimistic, set would be for senior management on the sales side. It is debatable whether any had more than a passing resemblance to reality.

At Jaguar, Robinson and his executives put together a detailed paper that presented the case for retaining Jaguar's autonomy. The arguments fell on deaf ears. Ken Edwards, then personnel director, comments: "We were disgusted at the way the Ryder people came in. We had prepared a presentation to show how Jaguar was doing and really, Ryder didn't want to know." Graham Whitehead, on the other hand, who now runs Jaguar's North American operations, recalls: "I talked to Ryder about our operations and Stanley Gillen did come to New York. He interviewed the US management and we had our Canadian president there. We discussed what we were doing and what the potential was for business."

An abridged version of the Ryder report was published on April 24, 1975. The conclusions ran to 51 paragraphs and included several points that caused grave concern at Jaguar. The report recommended for instance that BL's product development engineering team should be centralised. "We propose that the skills concerned with the various aspects of product development – product planning, styling engineering and vehicle engineering – should be brought within a single product development organisation for cars . . ." It was suggested that this organisation should be based at Solihull. For Jaguar, that could mean only one thing: that it would no longer be responsible for designing Jaguars. That was an appalling prospect. So far as Jaguar people were concerned, a car could be a true Jaguar only if it was styled, designed and built in their own factory at Browns Lane, Coventry. But there was more.

Chapter 12 of the report dealt with organisation and management. The team had considered four possible permutations. The first involved bringing all the car businesses into one integrated organisation – precisely what Lyons had opposed so vociferously during the negotiations between BMH and Leyland. Alternatively, three product divisions could be created: Austin-Morris, Rover-Triumph and Jaguar; that, in effect, meant that there would be no change from the arrangements that the report claimed were partly to blame for the company's current state. A third possibility was to create two divisions, one for volume cars, which would include Austin-Morris, the other for specialist cars, bringing together Jaguar and Rover-Triumph. That would have been more acceptable to Jaguar, as long as it dominated its group. The final option also involved two divisions: Austin, Morris, Rover and Triumph would be in one and Jaguar would form the other. This was, in fact, the arrangement that was finally implemented five years later. At the time, however, BL employees and industry observers claimed there was no logic to the proposal, since it would not involve a clear volume/specialist split. The fact that it was included was perhaps an indication of the effectiveness of Jaguar's lobbying.

The bad news came in paragraph 12.12. "We concluded that the creation of a single integrated car business as a separate profit centre within the corporation would best serve the interests of BL in the future." In that one sentence, so far as Jaguar people were concerned, Ryder had signed a death warrant for their company. The report conceded that there were strong arguments in favour of a separate identity for Jaguar – in particular, the need to preserve a separate identity for the marque and to maintain the loyalty of the employees. Even so, the Ryder team was convinced that BL's long-term future depended on an integrated organisation. To a degree, the staffs of the old companies, Austin-Morris, Rover-Triumph and Jaguar had only themselves to blame for this. Ever since the formation of BLMC, they had more or less gone their own ways. There had been little attempt to achieve inter-company co-ordination, and the Ryder report threw this back at them. "We do not consider that this arrangement (product based companies) has worked satisfactorily in the past, and it would be even less likely to operate satisfactorily if, as we believe is essential, the car divisions were genuinely separate profit centres."

Ken Edwards is adamant that Jaguar, at least, could have turned in a profit. "I know at that time, when the Ryder report was put out, we made £12 million profit."

Even so, it seems that Jaguar's attempts to retain autonomy had contributed to its losing it. The only crumb of comfort was the Report's statement that "BL should continue to produce both volume and specialist cars and should compete in all the major sectors of the car market, ranging from the small/light sector to the luxury sector . . ." At least there was still a role for Jaguar.

An organisation chart illustrated the new organisation proposed by the Ryder team. There would be a managing director, cars. Finance planning and control, systems, personnel, product planning, development and engineering, manufacturing, sales and marketing, parts and KD (knocked-down kits for export) would all report to him. Industrial relations came in for attention too, although the report denied that all the company's ills could be ". . . laid at the door of a strike-prone and work-shy labour force". This was undoubtedly true. The managers who had been running the group had to accept a large part of the blame for its failure. However, the report did show that, during the year ending September 30, 1970, nine million man hours had been lost through disputes. This had risen to 23.8 million man hours in 1974. In fact, time lost through stoppages at BL had risen almost twice as fast as in the rest of British industry over this period. Part of the reason must have been the complexity of the organisation. There were 170,000 employees in 60 plants run by eight divisions. Within those plants, there were 17 different unions.

In estimating the cost of the programme it proposed, the Ryder team pointed out that there had been a chronic lack of investment in new plant and equipment for many years. This would have to be put right at the same time as new products were developed. The cost of the capital investment that the team considered necessary was set at £1,264 million. When allowance was made for inflation, the figure rose to £2,090 million which would be needed by the end of September 1982. In addition, £260 million (£750 million adjusted for inflation) was needed as working capital. Most of the money would have to come from the government, since BL was not expected to achieve a positive cash flow until the financial year 1981–82.

The report made several forecasts on future sales. Some were remarkably accurate. The total UK car market would, it was suggested, be around 1.6 million units by 1980. In fact, it was 1.5 million. Ryder predicted that the market would grow to 1.7 million vehicles and possibly higher by 1985. The actual figure was 1.83

million. However, the team was less accurate in its forecasts of BL's market share: "BL should be able to retain in the early 1980s its present share of the UK market for cars. . . ." The reality was that, within five years, BL's share of the UK car market would fall to little more than half the 1974 figure.

Jaguar's market share had been running at around the 1 per cent from 1970 to 1975. The company had sold about 12,000 cars a year in the UK from 1969 to 1975, with two exceptional years. In 1971, 15,416 cars were sold. That was the first year in which the XJ saloons, announced in the autumn of 1968, were relatively freely available. In 1974, the year after the announcement of the Series 2 XJ saloon, the figure was 14,493. However the figures were interpreted, Jaguar was not likely to make much of a contribution to the sales volume and market share aspirations set out by Ryder. What it did do, however, was to make a significant contribution to profits, simply because a significant profit was made on every Jaguar or Daimler sold, at a time when there was virtually no profit in selling Minis. Geoffrey Robinson stresses: "It was the Jaguar franchise that kept Austin Morris alive in Europe and the rest of the world."

The report pointed out that, with sales of about 200,000 cars, BL had under 3 per cent of the European market. It was thought that that could grow. However, since the market was expected to grow to 10 million units in 1985, BL would have to increase its sales in Europe by half just to retain its market share. Even at the time, there were many who thought that Ryder was impossibly optimistic; some of them were within BLMC. Head of publicity Bob Berry was one of a group who wrote a paper strongly disagreeing with the report's projections. Stokes also disagreed with the figures. "The thing with the Ryder report, which was absolutely farcical, was the way they suddenly projected fantastic sales all over the world," he says. "They were just talking through the backs of their heads. They had no knowledge at all of the motor industry." Stokes acknowledges that sales forecasts produced within the company were always high. "You let these boys talk their figures and then you cut them down by 75 per cent if you had any sense."

The report was also closely examined by the House of Commons Expenditure Committee's trade and industry sub-committee, which was also highly sceptical. Albert Duffy, the Labour MP who chaired it, commented: "The Ryder team . . . put forward recommendations on the basis of assumptions that just cannot withstand serious scrutiny." The sub-committee pointed out that the report required BL to become "more profitable than any large European manufacturer" had ever been. It added that the possibility of splitting the group into independent truck and bus, quality car and volume car companies seemed not to have been seriously considered. Perhaps the sub-committee had Rolls-Royce in mind. When Rolls-Royce failed in 1971, Rolls-Royce Motors was formed as a separate company and later floated off by the receiver. Possibly the sub-committee thought the same could have been done with Jaguar.

In reality, that was unlikely. Rolls-Royce Motors had no real competition for its products. Jaguar was competing with several other manufacturers both in Britain and in important export markets. That meant Jaguar's pricing policy was more dictated by market conditions than that of Rolls-Royce Motors. It also meant Jaguar needed to update its product line more frequently, at a cost of millions. Given its sales performance, Jaguar's chances of earning sufficient profits to fund a substantial development programme were remote. More to the point, no one could say with certainty that the company was making a profit at all. The way in which BLMC prepared its figures precluded any extrapolation of profit or loss for Jaguar. Robinson remains convinced, however, that the company was profitable. "If you took the spares profit and the profit made on its sales abroad, it was always a profitable company," he says. John Edwards, the current Finance Director, is sure Jaguar made a profit every year until 1978. When he was preparing for the company's privatisation in 1984, he recreated the accounts for the missing years. "It was mainly in the order of £10 million in the early 1970s," he says. "1974 was about £12 million."

Profits from spares and overseas sales did not accrue to Jaguar under the BLMC regime. They went to other divisions, which greatly angered Robinson. "I didn't have control of the American market, I didn't have control of the European market," he says. "The only market that I did control was the UK. What the hell was I supposed to do? I used to 'phone up America, I used to have them over, but at the end of the day, they didn't report to me."

It is possible that Jaguar could have been sold to another manufacturer on the basis of its name alone, but the buyer would inevitably have been foreign, and the thought of selling one of Britain's most prestigious car makers to an overseas company must have been anathema to a Labour administration. Stokes had also rejected the idea of selling profitable parts of the group to raise cash. "The opportunity to sell it off never came up," he says today. "I don't recollect anybody wanting to buy it, but I would have been against it anyway, because Jaguar was a big contributor to the profits of the company."

In the same year the Ryder report was published, the government's Policy Review Staff, (the "think tank"), produced another report, *The Future of the British Motor Industry*. This concluded that there was likely to be severe competition in the European market owing to overcapacity, and it highlighted many short-comings among British manufacturers. There were, it claimed, ". . . too many manufacturers with too many models, too many plants and too much capacity . . ." Subsequent developments were to prove that the think tank had a better grasp of realities than the Ryder team.

Robinson admits that there was a superficial logic to Ryder's recommendations. "If all you want to do is stick to logic, then he had it. Ford existed and that was the way Ford was run. Mercedes-Benz, in a way, was run like that, but they were one-product companies. Then there was General Motors." Robinson's argument is that Ford and Mercedes-Benz both built a cohesive range under one product name. General Motors, on the other hand, had several marques which were each managed indepen-dently. According to Robinson, it was the General Motors model that should have been followed instead of that of Ford.

Trevor Taylor, who was sales operations manager on the

Austin-Morris side of the company, is one of many who felt that the Ryder recommendations could not be dismissed. "It did seem to us that all the companies were struggling and the sensible thing to do would be to try and put the thing together and get some rationalised product range out of it." Another sales executive, Malcolm Hart, expresses a slightly different view. "It was pretty obvious that we could survive and completely restructure the company and its product range only with substantial financial assistance. I think the feeling within the company was that it was very good news from our point of view because, at last, somebody had understood the basic need for cash to fund all the changes that would need to be undertaken."

Graham Whitehead saw Ryder as offering a solution when almost anything was better than nothing. "I don't think that I sat too long to consider whether it was the right thing to do or not," he says. "It was merely a plan, a recommendation, and it seemed better than the chaos that was existing before. Subsequently, clearly it was quite the wrong way to go, but I'm not sure that I felt particularly strongly against it at the time."

Regardless of the way the report was seen within the company, the government apparently believed everything it said. It is difficult to escape the conclusion that the report told the government what it wanted to hear. Even so, it seems remarkable that it was accepted as the blueprint for British Leyland's revival in the face of such a barrage of criticism. The British Leyland Bill was published on May 13; it allowed the government to buy the group's shares at 10p each. In the event, 90,000 shareholders chose to hang on, either in the hope that the value of their holding would rise or for sentimental reasons. On May 21, 1975, the guarantee was increased from £50 million to £100 million by Parliament.

One of the group's worst difficulties was its industrial relations record. Ryder attempted to attack this by calling for a three-tier employee participation plan that involved consultation with employees' representatives on new model and facility planning, sales and marketing plans and financial performance. This achieved little beyond introducing an unprecedented level of bureaucracy, with meetings being held by unions and management separately, to decide how they would approach the meetings held to decide the agenda of the employee participation meetings proper! Apart from that, it attacked the fundamental role of the managers – that of managing the company. Participation was about management by consensus rather than by skilled managers. Admittedly, few senior managers within BL had shown themselves to be particularly skilled in the past, but given the fact that many plants had convenors and shop stewards whose views and aspirations were quite different from any that would have been adopted by a responsible manager, achieving consensus often took many months.

Robinson believed in the concept, but most managers who had to work within the employee participation framework viewed it as an unwarranted intrusion. By enshrining the ideology in a set of laid down procedures, BL created a monster that hindered progress rather than creating a co-operative atmosphere that would help the company achieve its goals. There have been suggestions, too, that extreme left-wingers on the union side were less interested in the success of BL than in using it for their political ends. If that was true, then the employee participation scheme played directly into their hands by ensuring that the only communication channels between the boardroom and the factory floor were through them.

For Jaguar and Robinson, the group structure set out in the Ryder report had profound implications. It was clear that Jaguar was not to be autonomous; and there was no role for Robinson, who had, anyway, said that he would leave if Ryder called for complete integration. There had been speculation in the press that Robinson could become managing director of the car manufacturing division. That did not happen and it was never a real possibility, because Robinson had made powerful enemies. When he had developed his plan for expanding Jaguar, he had presented it to the board to gain approval for the necessary capital expenditure, but had been turned down. Robinson went ahead anyway. He claims that he had been "given the nod" to do this by Stokes and Barber. "Stokes and Barber said, yes, go ahead, commit on the long-lead items," he claims. "Then all of it suddenly went bust. We didn't have the capital sanctions through, and we'd committed. The steel arrived and they used that as an excuse."

Ken Edwards corroborates Robinson's version of events. "I used to spend quite a lot of time in Geoffrey's office," he says. "On one occasion, he got a call from John Barber about the paint shop. The impression that I got from that conversation . . . was that he actually got permission to go ahead on the long-lead items." Stokes, however, denies this. He claims the real problem was that there had been no competitive tendering process for the job of constructing the new paint plant. Whichever account is accurate, Ron Lucas was asked, as secretary to the board, to write a letter of censure to Robinson. With that episode still fresh in people's minds, Robinson had no future with the company, even if he had wanted to stay.

Nor was there a role for Robinson's Jaguar management board. Indeed, it is claimed that the unpublished part of the Ryder report containing commercially sensitive information, suggested that the Jaguar team should be disbanded quickly. Both Bob Knight, the engineering director, who was later to do so much to keep Jaguar separate, and Ken Edwards maintain that they were told this by insiders. "I understood that the report said the strongest team in BL was the Jaguar team," Edwards says. "It either ought to be allowed to run as a team or, if they were going to put all the car companies together, it should be dispersed to the four winds, because it would be difficult to amalgamate." That is what happened. The management board was disbanded and Robinson resigned in mid-1975.

Stokes became honorary president of British Leyland. Today, he admits that it would have been better if the company had had an independent chairman. "I would have much preferred to have continued on the sales side," he says. "Although I trained as an engineer, I am not interested in the production side of making motor cars. I like marketing and selling much better. I enjoyed it much better and I was much better at it. I didn't know about any of the vast production problems of Austin-Morris. All I could do was try to hire the best people I could, but it was very difficult to hire anybody who had experience, very difficult indeed."

As attempts were made to implement the Ryder report, resentments built up within the operating companies. Organisation charts began to circulate with a few names appearing in senior positions. Other boxes were marked TBA (to be appointed) which was interpreted at Jaguar and Rover-Triumph as meaning "To Be Austin". The belief was widespread that top jobs would be filled by people from the volume car division. At Jaguar, there was no confidence that they would understand the company or its products.

CHAPTER 2
Killing the Cat

In the immediate aftermath of the Ryder report, there was confusion and uncertainty throughout the group. A new structure emerged in the course of the summer of 1975. BLMC was transmogrified into British Leyland Ltd, with four divisions: Leyland Cars – including Jaguar – Leyland Truck and Bus, Leyland Special Products and Leyland International. Stokes was shunted upstairs as honorary president of the new company, and Alex Park became chief executive. Derek Whittaker was appointed chief executive of Leyland Cars. For Jaguar, these developments brought little comfort. Relatively few Jaguar people were appointed to senior jobs in the new organisation. It was inevitable that they would be outnumbered because there had been only a handful of them to start with. Nevertheless, the absorption of Jaguar's sales and marketing effort by Leyland Cars was seen as another nail in the coffin, particularly since the team was based at Longbridge from late summer.

As if to emphasise that Jaguar was no longer autonomous, the launch of the XJ-S was handled by the new organisation. In the past, new Jaguars had been announced to dealers at meetings held either at the main factory at Browns Lane, or at prestigious hotels. But when the XJ-S was announced, the dealers were called to Longbridge, home of Austin. The psychological effect of such a step on Jaguar employees is difficult for outsiders to understand. Longbridge was within the group, but for Jaguar it was foreign territory. It was as if a British monarch had been crowned in Washington DC. One Midlands distributor recalls the event as "the ultimate damnation".

It was easy to justify the decision on purely economic grounds. The presentation of a new car to dealers is usually a theatrical affair. Slides, film and company spokesmen alternate in a show that builds up to the great climactic moment – the unveiling of the new car. It is more expensive to use outside facilities for these shows, and with money so tight, it was decided to stage a factory event for the XJ-S. The choice was between Browns Lane and Longbridge.

Both sites had exhibition halls. The one at Browns Lane was normally used to display historic cars and had a flat floor. The Longbridge facility had been used for car launches for years; it had a stage with three turntables built into it, as well as cinema screens and seating. All of these would have had to be installed if the show had taken place at Browns Lane. In addition, Longbridge had a large catering area alongside the exhibition hall. The catering facilities at Browns Lane were much smaller and so a marquee would have been needed to provide lunch for the dealers. Nevertheless, the belief persists that the new management wanted to demonstrate that it called the shots at Jaguar.

The event was arranged by Austin-Morris people, many of whom lacked any knowledge of Jaguar and its products. Further proof of that was provided when the XJ-S was announced to the public at the Duckhams Birmingham Motoring Festival in September 1975. The Lord Mayor of Birmingham presided and when he looked under the bonnet, he asked the company representative standing nearby, a long-standing Austin-Morris employee, where the carburettors were. He was told that they were out of sight. Someone else had to explain that the car had fuel injection and so there were no carburettors.

That year brought another example of the upstaging of Browns Lane. Ralph Broad ran a motor racing team from Southam in Warwickshire, and he suggested to Jaguar that he should prepare and race an XJ-S with their support. To gain maximum publicity from the project, the Jaguar would have had to beat the BMWs that were winning in the group 2 saloon car championship. But the XJ-S did not meet the criteria laid down by the international motor racing authorities for this category, and the Jaguar engineers had their hands full developing new models. They could spare no time to help Broad, and they did not believe the XJ-S could have been a winner without considerable work.

Undeterred, Broad went to the BL management and persuaded them that racing success would bring the group useful publicity. They agreed to help him to develop a racing version of the XJ 2-door coupé, without involving Jaguar at all. Broad began work on the car and, in early 1976, the programme was announced. Two cars were developed, but they achieved little beyond appearing on the track. They were heavy by racing standards, so that extensive work on the brakes was necessary. Once these were capable of slowing the car from racing speeds, engine lubrication became a problem. Then the wheels and hubs began to give trouble under the high cornering forces. The programme became a succession of obstacles that could not be overcome quickly enough to meet BL management's aspirations. At the end of the 1977 season, it was cancelled, having created a considerable amount of ill-will at Jaguar. The cars had appeared in seven races and, although they had frequently been fastest in practice and had led every race for varying periods, the best result was a second place at Nürburgring in Germany. In the eyes of Jaguar the company had been held up to ridicule, an unforgivable sin.

In July 1977, Broad proposed that a syndicate should enter an XJ-S in the 1978 Le Mans race, and that the Jaguar V12 engine could be converted to diesel fuel for fast marine use. Neither suggestion was taken up.

A Jaguar operating committee was formed in June 1975, chaired by Tony Thompson, who had been put in charge of all BL's large car assembly operations: Jaguar, Rover at Solihull and Vanden Plas. This was one of the more incomprehensible decisions in the post-Ryder period. Whereas Ryder had envisaged a single car manufacturing entity, what was created was a series of almost arbitrary groupings of manufacturing facilities. The arrangement lasted less than a year. The Jaguar operating committee was formed as a device to avert criticism of the new group organisation. It was hailed by the press as evidence that the company was to retain its autonomy. However, a more important development was announced at the same time.

By this time, Bob Knight was chief engineer at Jaguar and should have reported to Spen King, had the Ryder report been implemented in full. King had been in charge of engineering at Rover-Triumph and was now responsible for the new central engineering and development department. Knight had no intention of reporting to King and lobbied, among others, Ryder himself. According to Knight, Ryder told him: "Nothing in that report's written in tablets of stone." Knight had mastered the skills of corporate politics at least as well as his opponents, and a good deal better than some. And he had one weapon that none of them could match: he possessed the ability to wear them down through painstaking attention to detail. One former colleague recalls going to see him on an internal matter. "If it had been anyone else, I suppose we might have spent an hour or so discussing it," he recalls. "But with Bob, it took us three days to cover the details to his satisfaction."

Jim Randle, Knight's successor as engineering director, says Knight ". . . had an ability to hold people at bay, intellectually hold people at bay to the point where they just got so fed up with the darn thing that they would leave him alone. He often said, 'You don't make decisions, you ultimately come to conclusions,' which is right. If you work at it long enough, that's what happens, but you have to grind through a whole mass of detail to get there." Another of Knight's maxims was: "You break things down into fundamentals and you apply logic." Randle explains: "You'd sit in his office for hours and hours while he ground through the detail, often on a subject that was your speciality. By the time he got half-way through this grinding process, you began to see something that he was going to get to which you hadn't covered. You knew it was only a matter of time before he got there, which helped your thinking process quite a lot."

Knight himself claims that he won the fight to retain Jaguar engineering as a separate entity by ". . . fighting with cars; my main ally was the Jaguar motor car." Success depended on "the esteem in which it was held within the hierarchy". Doubtless there is something in that but there is no doubt either, that the prospect of endless sessions discussing the minutiae of organisational proposals was sufficient to deter most potential adversaries. So Knight successfully defended Jaguar engineering from the Ryder assault.

In doing so, he helped to ensure the survival of Jaguar itself. But Knight's achievement was matched, in the factory, by Peter Craig, the plant director. Craig had been with Jaguar since 1941, working his way up through the factory. He fought to retain a distinct identity for Jaguar under the Leyland Cars organisation, but died in February 1977, before he could see the results of his work.

In January 1976, Tony Thompson was made responsible for all Leyland Cars vehicle assembly. In addition to Jaguar, Rover and Vanden Plas, he now had the unenviable task of overseeing the activities of Triumph at Liverpool (Speke) and Coventry (Canley), Austin at Longbridge, Morris at Cowley, MG at Abingdon and Seneffe, the Group's assembly plant in Belgium. This motley collection of factories employed more than 45,000 people and produced between 19,000 and 20,000 vehicles a week. Thompson was succeeded in February 1977 by David Simpson.

Simpson recalls attempts to overcome various problems at Jaguar. "There was a divide between production and engineering," he says. "I started holding meetings where I got everybody together. It wasn't very popular, but we had to get an understanding that engineering solutions weren't always suitable to production." This has been a long-running battle within car companies, not only Jaguar. Engineers tend to believe that production people are incapable of building well designed components, while production people complain that engineers do not understand the complexities of manufacturing. Simpson maintains that he began the process of encouraging each group to understand the other's problems.

He also claims to have made progress on enhancing quality. "A lot of quality improvements were put in place at that time," he says. "Wind noise problems were attacked and other fundamental defects." While Simpson was attempting to bring about change at Browns Lane, the sales and marketing staff for the whole of Leyland Cars was installed in a new office block in Redditch, Worcestershire during the summer of 1976, and it was here that an attempt was made to turn the company into a market-driven organisation. Critics had maintained for years that the component companies of what became Leyland Cars were production-led.

Successes like the Mini had been due to inspiration, rather than to a careful analysis of market demands. To an extent, that was also true of Jaguar, although Lyons's instincts had again and again proved more accurate than those of Austin-Morris chairmen. It was decided that a central marketing organisation had to be created. The man appointed to lead it was Cedric Scroggs.

Scroggs came to Leyland Cars from Cadbury, and set about building a team of four marketing managers. His intention, which followed classical marketing precepts, was that each marketing manager should be responsible for the annual profit of the models under his or her control. This represented a massive change of direction for Leyland Cars, not least because it would involve identifying the profit contribution from each product range. At the time, no one appears to have had the remotest idea how much profit was made on each car. Prices were determined not on a cost-plus basis but by what the market would bear and how the cars compared with competitive models from other manufacturers. Thus, a Jaguar had to be priced to compete with a Mercedes. But no one knew how much it cost to build a Jaguar. Consequently, no one could say for certain whether any profit was being made, much less tell a marketing manager how much profit each car contributed.

When Ray Horrocks joined the company as managing director of Austin-Morris in 1978, he found that for most of the products, there was not an authenticated bill of material. "Without that," he explains, "you can't add up the costs of the bits you're putting into a car, let alone the costs of labour." Scroggs was not aware of these problems when he joined the company. He had assumed that accurate figures would be available, but found that profit was not often discussed in the sales and marketing organisation. He believes this was largely because nobody had enough information to see what had an impact on profit and what did not. At that time, and for years afterwards, the sales and marketing management was entirely preoccupied with selling cars, as fast as possible and by any means possible. Volume and market penetration were the goals, profit being barely considered.

However, Scroggs set about appointing marketing managers.

Of these, one had responsibility for Jaguar, which was seen by the management of the time as just one model in the overall Leyland Cars range. "It was seen as being the luxury end of the range, above Rover, competing with the larger Mercedes and BMW models," he says. One of the early tasks of the new marketing department was to educate Leyland Cars executives in the principles of marketing. In this, Scroggs and his team faced an uphill task, largely because of events immediately after 1945.

Like many British manufacturing concerns, the companies that were to come together to form British Leyland had found themselves at that time in a sellers' market. The American motor industry was fully stretched trying to satisfy home demand, and had little inclination to tackle export markets. European manufacturers were rebuilding their factories and the Japanese had yet to develop as a world power in car manufacturing. The British government set out to earn foreign currency by encouraging manufacturers to export as much as 75 per cent of their production. They did this by continuing the rationing of steel, allocating most of it to production of export goods. For a time, British car makers effectively had export markets to themselves. They worked flat out to deliver as many cars as possible. Quality was not a concern. As one executive puts it: "People worked on the basis that some foreign fellow would put it right once it arrived."

Nor was much concern paid to local preferences. The concept of marketing was unknown, for everything that could be built could be sold, both at home and abroad. Even at Ford, the first car manufacturer to adopt marketing techniques, senior marketing staff tended to be American as late as the 1960s for the simple reason that no experienced British marketing people were to be found. British manufacturing companies began to pay the price of years of ruling an empire. They had become accustomed to telling the natives what was good for them, but as the empire began to shrink, the new nations decided that they wanted to make their own choices. The British proved unable to adapt to a changing world.

When Scroggs arrived at Leyland Cars, manufacturing people were in control. The people who ran the factories regarded the newcomers with derision: they were dubbed "flower arrangers". It was against this background that, in July 1976, Scroggs made a presentation to senior managers on the role of consumer research in the early stages of new model development. The thrust of his argument was that the company had to produce cars that customers would buy; to do that, it had first to establish what those customers wanted. One way to find out is by means of "styling clinics" where potential buyers are shown full-size replicas of cars being developed. These clinics often take place years before a new car is launched, and important decisions on styling are made on the basis of customer reaction. Judging by the comments of senior directors as much as six months after Scroggs's presentation, car clinics were viewed with extreme scepticism within the company.

Scroggs points out that several important issues were at stake. There was the gap between the market share targets that had been declared for political reasons and the reality of the market place. He maintains that there was no forum for discussing this. Then there were such questions as the varying acceptability of hatchback cars as against those with boots, crucial for the product plan. "These were central matters, and yet we might as well have been talking Martian to many senior managers, who appeared not to grasp the importance of finding out what the consumer wanted."

That might seem a severe criticism but, as Scroggs himself acknowledges, the structure of the company created enormous difficulties. The Ryder report had designed a corporation to be run by autocrats, yet the people who were installed at the top were not autocratic. The byzantine structure meant that the only point at which departments of Leyland Cars met was, effectively, the managing director's desk. "Derek Whittaker alone convened any meetings at which really serious discussion took place of what to do," says Scroggs. "He was constantly under pressure from group headquarters in London. The political pressures were immense. The industrial relations pressures on him must have been extraordinary. All those pressures took the eye of top management off the ball." Under the circumstances, it is not surprising that Scroggs's plans for the future should have been subordinated to the arguments about what to do to solve immediate problems.

By this time, Jaguar played only a minor role in the company. Not only was it marked down as little more than a model, in much the same way as Ford has its Granada at the top of the range, but responsibility for sales continued to be divided. Geoffrey Robinson had complained bitterly about having no control over export sales. The new organisation still divided sales between two separate divisions: Leyland Cars, which was responsible for UK sales, and Leyland International. Ryder had recommended this division, which was unique in the industry and caused much ill feeling. Because the manufacturing organisation had no responsibility for overseas sales and marketing, it was able to blame the International staff for poor performance. International accused the factories of supply shortfalls, and so the arrangement effectively set up two warring factions. Perhaps more important was the fact that the division of responsibilities meant no one at an operational level had a complete picture. Whittaker was responsible for Leyland Cars, but had no brief for Leyland International.

Towards the end of 1976, a new spectre began to haunt the company that was of profound concern to Jaguar. Discussion at a high level within Leyland Cars began to centre on the idea of renaming all the company's products Leyland, with marque names used to denote individual models. Jaguars would become Leyland Jaguars. The argument rumbled on for 12 months, and was only brought to an end when Michael Edwardes joined the company in November 1977.

The rationale for the proposal was that Leyland Cars was a single entity and that its products should be identified with the company. In Europe, it was pointed out, the individual marque names were not well known, and neither was the Leyland name. Thus a corporate identity could be built around the name of Leyland. It was pointed out that in Britain, the name Leyland was associated with trucks and strikes. There was a risk that the whole car range would be branded with Leyland's troubles. Eventually, it was decided to retain individual marque names, but to add the Leyland logo to car badging. By various means, Jaguar managed to avoid even that. Name boards outside the plants, however, were a different matter.

In the name of corporate identity, manufacturing plants had been given new titles. The signs at Browns Lane read "Leyland Cars Large Car Assembly Plant". What the theoreticians overlooked or ignored was the fact that the people at Browns Lane built Jaguars, and were proud of the fact. They did not assemble large cars for Leyland and resented the new signs, suspecting that there was a sinister purpose behind them. In an effort to overcome the antagonism that had been created, it was suggested that the words "the home of Jaguar cars" shoud be added. It was never done, and such a gesture would in any case have had little effect on the workforce. The old Daimler factory at Radford became known as Radford Engines and Transmission Plant.

Signs were not the only point of contention. Browns Lane and Radford were managed separately, and co-ordination between the two was made increasingly difficult. Far from simplifying management, the Ryder plan was making life more complicated, particularly in engineering. In Leyland Cars as a whole, the four major development functions – chassis, body, power unit and transmission and electrical – operated independently, reporting separately to one central director. Fortunately, this arrangement was avoided at Jaguar, although not without a considerable amount of manoeuvring.

Under the circumstances, it is not suprising that rumours began to circulate that Jaguar production was to move to the Rover factory at Solihull. Whether that was ever a serious possibility is not clear, but it is quite likely that it was considered. Solihull had a new factory, built to produce the Rover 3500, code-named SD1. It was more modern than Browns Lane and had sufficient capacity to build both Rovers and Jaguars. If the BL board aimed to reduce the number of factories, closing Browns Lane was an option. It never happened, but the rumours further lowered the morale at Jaguar.

The same centralisation strategy was employed among the dealers. Trevor Taylor, who by this time was sales director for Leyland Cars, explains: "Our directive from the board was to create a single franchise under the Leyland Cars umbrella, and to integrate Rover, Triumph, Austin, Morris, Jaguar, Daimler, Land Rover and Range Rover under a single franchise line. In overall terms, that didn't make much sense, so what we did was to create a base-line franchise – Austin-Morris. Everybody had to sell them. Separate franchising studies said that we needed about 250 Jaguar dealers." The Jaguar franchise, then, was "bolted on" to the Austin-Morris franchise in some areas. The rules precluded a dealer holding only a Jaguar franchise.

It is true that the rules were bent on occasion. Where a dealer had been successful in selling one of the specialist marques, he had now, theoretically, to take on Austin-Morris. But some dealers were totally unsuited to selling volume cars, and were given a "nil allocation". This meant that, although they carried the Austin-Morris sign on their showrooms, they never received any Austin-Morris cars to sell. It was one way of retaining successful Jaguar dealers.

Jaguar was seen as a profitable franchise to hold, unlike Austin-Morris. The result was that, just as special cases were made for some dealers, Jaguar was used as a bargaining token with others. If a dealer was reluctant to keep the Austin-Morris franchise in an important area, he was offered Jaguar as well. Nor was this the only example of Jaguar being used to shore up Austin-Morris. When the company's sales staff negotiated contracts with dealers for supplies of cars, Jaguars were used as an incentive for them to accept an increased allocation of models that were more difficult to sell.

This policy created almost as many problems as it solved. The increase in the number of Jaguar dealers meant that the supply of cars was spread very thinly. In some cases, a dealer might be allocated only three XJ-S models each year, yet a considerable investment in spares, service equipment and technician training was needed in order to provide a good after-sales service for the car, with its V12 engine. The volume of cars did not justify that investment, so the standard of service in some outlets was far below the level that owners expected.

The same considerations that led to Jaguars being used as bait for dealers lay behind a suggestion in 1977 that Leyland Cars could be made more profitable if it concentrated on building cars for the more lucrative end of the market. This proposal, contained in a paper produced by Leyland Cars marketing department as an alternative to the 1977 business plan, would have meant concentrating on Jaguar, Rover, Land Rover and Range Rover because of their assumed higher unit profitability. It would also have meant abandoning the Metro, which was under development, and reducing the scope of models in the Maestro and Montego ranges, then in the early planning stages. Although the profit per vehicle was not known, it was obvious that one Jaguar contributed more than a handful of Minis.

The plan was never a realistic proposition because it would have involved closing the Longbridge body and assembly factories, Cowley north works and the TR7 plant in Loverpool, and transferring manufacture of the TR7 to the MG plant at Abingdon. The number of people employed in the manufacturing plants would have been reduced from the 1976 level of 129,700 to 89,100 by 1986. Politically, this would have been quite unacceptable at the time. At the October 1974 general election, Labour had won a five-seat majority, and the wholesale closure of big manufacturing plants would have made the government's position even more difficult.

Even so, there was an attempt to convince union leaders that Jaguar would play a major role in Leyland Cars. At a meeting in March 1977 of senior group directors and local officials of all the major trade unions represented in British Leyland, plans were outlined that would bring Jaguar production up to 1,200 a week within 10 years. This would require capital investment of £142 million. These production figures seem optimistic even today; the company was a long way from achieving that level of output by the end of 1986.

The unions, plainly, needed to be reassured about Jaguar's long-term future. At the same time, Cedric Scroggs was still trying, not always successfully, to convince Jaguar management that he had its interests at heart. At one stage, the Jaguar marketing manager was denied sight of early styling exercises aimed at developing a new saloon to replace the XJ6. It is true that such styling themes are highly confidential, but the marketing manager could not have been expected to begin to develop plans for the new car if he did not know what it looked like. Under the terms of Scroggs's brief, his department should also have been involved in the design and specification of the new car. Without sight of the plans, this was obviously impossible. In this instance, the Jaguar managers were fighting a friend. "I had a particular interest in Jaguar," Scroggs says, "partly because I thought it was being neglected to a degree that was risky."

One of the reasons for that neglect was that the sales people were under intense pressure to move the volume cars. Politically, the company was under pressure because its market share was consistently below the level that had been publicly declared as a target. The easiest way to try to regain that level was to promote the models that sold in the greatest quantities. As one senior manager of the time puts it: "We had so many problems in trying to maintain market share for the volume cars that Jaguar had to bumble along on its own. It was such tiny numbers, relatively speaking, that no one really cared or thought about it. That does sound dreadful and I'm slightly ashamed of saying it, but that's the truth of the matter." According to this view, which is shared by many, Jaguar was left to look after itself, not as a conscious policy, but simply because its levels of sales had little impact on the market penetration of Leyland Cars as a whole.

Trevor Taylor was, by this time, in charge of sales for all Leyland Cars products. He denies vehemently that Jaguar was neglected. "I got booted in the arse if I failed to achieve the Jaguar objectives," he says. "We were selling the whole range. We were just as concerned, believe me, about selling Jaguars and they were bloody tough. They were very, very hard to move, have no doubts about that."

One of the men who was resonsible for computing the figures that told the factories what to build points to a further problem: "Jaguar's misfortune was to be bottom of the list," he says. At that time, he would begin working out production figures at the beginning of the price list. "We'd begin crunching through the numbers at Mini 850. When we reached Jaguar, we'd run out of time." The implication is that less attention was paid to planning production volumes for Jaguar than for the volume cars.

Time was often an enemy. The Series III Jaguar XJ6 was under development and was badly needed, but its story is one of missed deadlines. There were problems with the electric aerial, the optional sunshine roof and the fuel injection. The car was originally to have been launched at the UK Motor Show in October 1977, but it was evident from April that that date was unrealistic. The launch did not take place until the following March. It might not have mattered much had the delays not become public knowledge. The fact that they did, meant that potential customers began to postpone purchases, preferring to wait for the new model. UK sales fell to 9,387 cars, the lowest since the end of the 1950s.

The sales and marketing department realised that nothing could be done about the missed deadlines, but asked that the delays be used to good effect by spending more time testing the Series III. The XJ6, in particular its electrical systems, had developed a reputation for unreliability, and it was considered vital that the worst faults should be eliminated from the Series III by the time it was launched. When the car appeared, however, it was no more reliable than its predecessor.

The sales people were particularly disappointed that the Series III was initially available only in red, yellow and white. New cars are frequently launched with a limited range of colours, so that in itself was not disastrous. These particular colours, however, had been developed for the Rover 3500 and it was felt that they were unsuitable for the Jaguar. According to one dealer, even that did not matter too much, but 18 months later the colour range had still not been extended.

Looking back, Scroggs admits that his department had little effect on Leyland Cars, and that is hardly surprising. He was faced with an impossible task. The manufacturing staff had held sway for too long to be prepared to listen to outsiders lacking direct experience of the car business. At Jaguar, the antagonism was even worse: not only was the marketing manager from outside the industry, he also worked for Leyland Cars. He had little chance of influencing decisions taken by manufacturing or engineering, and so was never much more than a co-ordinator of advertising and promotional campaigns aimed at selling the cars Jaguar produced. The company was still following the age-old practice of building cars and then telling the sales people to sell them.

Nor did the marketing department enjoy the respect of the sales organisation. As one dealer put it: "The rumours were that Scroggs and Trevor Taylor had endless head to heads." Both deny this now, but it is obvious that there was resentment between the two departments. Both reported to the head of Leyland Cars sales and marketing organisation, Keith Hopkins. Thus, on paper, the sales operation and the marketing team met only at the head. Each team had different objectives. For the sales department, the priority was to get cars sold as quickly as possible. Marketing, on the other hand, seemed more concerned with long term objectives. So it was left to the sales department to devise tactical campaigns designed to win immediate sales.

Jaguar's pride continued to suffer regular buffets. The main showcase for any car manufacturer in Britain is the Motor Show. In 1976 this was still being held at Earl's Court, in London, and it was here that Jaguar was, again, publicly integrated with the rest of the Leyland Cars range.

Even in the days of BMH, Jaguar had had its own Motor Show stand, and the practice had been continued during the BLMC period. In 1976, however, Jaguars and Daimlers were lined up alongside Marinas and Minis on a open stand. People could walk up to any car and sit in it if they wished. It is difficult entirely to justify the antagonism felt by many die-hard Jaguar people to this arrangement. Under Lyons, the company had always had open stands, in contrast to some of its competitors, who protected their cars behind barriers that would be opened only to the chosen few. As Bob Berry, the former Jaguar PR chief, explains: "Sir William Lyons believed that, even if it was an 11-year-old boy sitting in the driving seat, that experience might well create in him, the aspiration to own one when he was old enough." Robinson had tried to introduce a closed stand, but had been persuaded to stay with the open concept by, among others, Berry. "It's a Motor Show," explains Berry. "People have paid to come in, and they should have access to the products they have come to see."

The cries of horror from Jaguar people were caused by the juxtaposition of Jaguars with the more prosaic offerings from other parts of the group. It was felt to be an offence against their prestige and exclusivity. There appear to have been two reasons for the arrangement: the new management wanted the group to be seen as an integrated concern. There was even a television commercial showing all of British Leyland's cars, including Jaguars and Daimlers. Just as important, however, was the question of cost. A Motor Show stand is extremely expensive to design and build. It was undoubtedly cheaper to have one stand rather than two, and money was still very tight. So the decision could be defended on several grounds, but it still served to fuel antipathy between Jaguar and the rest of Leyland Cars.

More important than Jaguar's pride, however, was the fact that the quality of cars coming off the production lines was appalling. There were several reasons for this. First was the low morale brought about by the actions of the BL management. Just as damaging was the drive for increased production, which resulted in poorly fitting body panels, dreadful paint finish and rushed assembly. Dealers often had to carry out extensive work on new cars before they could be delivered. Even so, the cars that were reaching customers had badly fitting body panels and trim and were unreliable. Part of that unreliability was blamed on outside suppliers, though present and past executives refuse to be specific. But while the quality of components from some suppliers was certainly poor, Jaguar at times appeared to have little interest in ensuring that the design of components was right in the first place. Engineering director Bob Knight tended to be more concerned with future models than the current cars. Unreliability pushed up warranty costs, which became a drain on profits and led many customers to lose faith in Jaguars.

The extent of the problem had been suggested by the 1976

National Car Quality Tracking Study in America. This showed that the average number of faults on newly delivered Jaguars was 5.79 per car, compared with an average of 2.96 on BMWs. Yet even this did not give the full picture. The study, and the warranty claims, showed only those items that actually failed. One of the problems with Jaguars was that some components, while not actually failing, did not function properly. So owners were often dissatisfied, but could get no redress; such cases did not show in any statistics. The effect was to undermine Jaguar's future sales potential. The tracking study showed that only 27 per cent of Jaguar owners intended to buy another, whereas 60 per cent of BMW owners were prepared to remain loyal to their marque.

There seems to have been considerable reluctance on the part of senior people at Jaguar to acknowledge that quality standards were too low. One of the sales people recalls taking a representative from a company that was running around 14 Jaguars to Browns Lane to discuss faults in their cars. "These cars were off the road so often that the customer was becoming fed up. We'd done everything we could to sort it out and took them to Browns Lane as a last resort." The senior Jaguar man present claimed that the complaints were merely a series of "minor problems". The reaction was fierce. "They may be minor problems to you," said the customer, "but they've kept our cars off the road for far too long." He stormed out, and not long afterwards his company switched to Mercedes.

Unreliability was not limited to Jaguar. It occurred throughout BL's car manufacturing activities, and Charles Maple was appointed to find ways of building better quality into the products. A programme called Quality 77 was announced, designed to raise the awareness of everyone on the factory floor of the need for improvement. It was, however, little more than a cosmetic exercise. Notices appeared in the factories stressing the need for better quality. A film called *The Quality Connection* attempted to drive home the message in a dramatic fashion. Yet little evidence of improvement emerged. The flaw in the programme was that it suggested quality could be "inspected into" cars. In reality, cars have to be designed so as to ensure that quality is built in from the start. Inspection should be no more than confirmation that everything is being done correctly. The malaise was too deep rooted for Quality 77 to work.

In the two years after the Ryder report, enormous damage was done to Jaguar, both in terms of the people at the factory and in the market place. Nor was the picture much better in the rest of BL. It became clear that the Ryder Plan was unworkable. Lord Ryder (as he had by then become) took on the role of an outside executive. He visited the group's factories, talking directly to managers and union leaders; in so doing he undermined the people who had been appointed to run the group. He was meting out to them the same treatment that they had given to Jaguar. But his methods were singularly unsuccessful. The group's industrial relations record deteriorated, in spite of the much-vaunted employee participation scheme.

Cedric Scroggs is particularly critical of that programme. "As a communications process, it was a disaster, as a management process, it was laughable," he says. "You don't communicate with a workforce that way. I distinctly remember negotiating with a shop steward on whether it was permissible to hire secretaries from outside the company." Meanwhile, the group was sliding towards financial failure again, and suffered the worst industrial dispute in its history. Car manufacturing involves a wide range of different people, some skilled, many not. Toolroom workers had always considered themselves to be the cream of the workforce, owing to the highly skilled nature of their jobs. They claimed pay differentials had been eroded and sought to re-establish them. They also felt that they were not being properly represented in the complex web of pay bargaining and so began to demand separate negotiating rights through their unofficial toolroom committee. The company refused to recognise the committee, because it knew that if it did, other bargaining groups would spring up all over the organisation. The pay negotiating network was already hideously complicated and it needed to be simplified, not made even worse. Nor did the toolroom committee gain any encouragement from its own union, the Amalgamated Union of Engineering Workers (AUEW), which also refused to recognise it.

In February 1977, about 3,000 men in 11 different plants went on strike, causing 40,000 assembly workers to be laid off. Eric Varley, then Secretary of State for Industry, froze government funds for the company, and the board stated publicly that it would not ask the government for more money until the strike was settled. The toolroom men were told that, since they were on an unofficial strike, they would be sacked unless they returned to work. That threat brought the strike to an end after it had lasted a month. The company made no concessions.

During the stoppage, the government took another step along the road to employee participation. Each of the three big manufacturers, Leyland Cars, Ford and Vauxhall, was asked to arrange a conference with representatives of the management, the unions and the government present. Leyland Cars was chosen as the first. On February 11, Varley addressed an audience of Leyland Cars managers and shop stewards. He was then joined on stage by Jack Jones, general secretary of the Transport and General Workers' Union, AUEW president Hugh Scanlon, Derek Whittaker and Alex Park. The audience was given the opportunity to ask questions and the event was recorded on video tape. Films of it were distributed to all the group's factories so that every employee could see what had happened. The exercise achieved little and was never repeated.

When the toolmakers' strike was over, Varley asked the National Enterprise Board to report yet again on BL's future. This time, the government was told that progress was being made and that the next tranche of funds should be released. Once again, however, the view expressed was impossibly optimistic. The longer-term picture was of declining market share, increasing competition, poor productivity and a dealer network that was growing more insecure almost by the day.

In 1977, Ryder resigned as chairman of the NEB and was replaced by Leslie Murphy. This appointment marked a change of direction for the board. In his book *Back from the Brink*, Michael Edwardes explains that, under Ryder, the NEB board, of which he was a member, had little influence on decisions about BL. He describes how on one occasion he called on Sir Richard

Dobson, then chairman of BAT Industries and a fellow board member, to be told that Dobson had been asked to take on the chairmanship of BL. Edwardes had seen Ryder only the day before, and was astonished that he had been told nothing of the approach to Dobson.

Murphy's style was different. Edwardes recalls: "Post-Ryder, the NEB became more genuinely involved, and it didn't take long for its members' views on Leyland to emerge – changes at the top were a pre-requisite to the company's survival. Most of us saw that even with board and management changes the Ryder plan could not be executed successfully; the first thing to do was to establish a team at British Leyland who would face up to and define the more limited objectives which were clearly needed."

The difficulties Murphy faced were daunting. BL was again teetering on the brink of insolvency, and there was no possibility of channelling more funds through parliament before the end of the current session. The banks would have to be persuaded to help, and they would want strong assurances about the company's top management. If someone new was to be brought in, and everyone at the NEB seemed agreed that that was necessary, it had to be someone who knew BL. There was no time for learning. Murphy's solution was to turn to Edwardes.

CHAPTER 3
Halting the Decline

Edwardes arrived at BL on November 1 1977. Born in 1930, he had spent his early years in South Africa, where he studied law at Rhodes University, Grahamstown. He formed his first company at the age of 20 to lay out sports fields at a local school. A chance encounter with H. V. Schofield, a director of Chloride, brought the offer of a two-year management trainee placing in Chloride's London head office. Edwardes spent two years in Britain before returning to South Africa and a job with the Cape Battery Company; subsequently he rejoined Chloride as assistant sales manager in South Africa.

In 1963, he was transferred to Salisbury, Rhodesia, (now Harare, Zimbabwe) with the task of reorganising Chloride's interests throughout central Africa. Soon after Ian Smith's regime in Southern Rhodesia unilaterally declared its independence from Britain in 1965, Edwardes was persuaded by Chloride's chairman to return to Britain. He was first given the task of restructuring the group's nickel cadmium battery business in Redditch, Worcestershire. Once he had done that, he joined the main board, although he was still only 39.

He was put in charge of the restructuring of Chloride's Exide battery subsidiary, and increased Exide's profits from £600,000 a year to £5 million a year within 18 months. Shortly after this success, he was appointed chief executive of Chloride; in 1974, he took over as executive chairman. Between 1971 and 1977, when he joined BL on secondment, Chloride's pre-tax profits rose from £3.5 million to £26 million. Edwardes was, clearly, a highly successful businessman who had ample experience of restructuring companies. His approach was quite different to that of any other chairman appointed by the NEB. One of the conditions that he had laid down before accepting the job was that he was to have executive authority. So far as he was concerned, he was in charge and, although he would be answerable to the NEB, he would accept no interference from it.

Edwardes is a remarkable man. Although of small stature, he has a very powerful personality. In the years of his chairmanship, he proved himself to be an excellent communicator and to be capable of motivating people. An example of his skill was seen in February 1978 at Chesworth Grange hotel, Kenilworth. More than 700 union representatives from all over the company had been brought there to hear Edwardes explain his plans for the recovery of BL. They knew that he would want to cut jobs and when he entered the room, the atmosphere was hostile. Edwardes took off his jacket and talked for over an hour, outlining the difficulties facing the company and indicating how he intended to overcome them.

The essence of his message was that the company had to shed 12,000 jobs that year out of a total of 195,000. The group was to be split into Austin-Morris, Jaguar-Rover-Triumph, BL Components, Leyland Vehicles (the truck and bus business) and SP Industries, which would be the repository for several companies such as Coventry Climax and Aveling Barford. One purpose was to make possible rebuilding of marque loyalties which had been eroded during the Leyland Cars period. The holding company's name would be changed to BL Ltd and return the Leyland name to what Edwardes regarded as its proper place, on the front of a range of trucks. At the end of the conference, a vote of confidence was called for and the audience gave Edwardes their overwhelming support.

He also made a considerable impact at a more personal level. One manager who met him early in 1978 described him as ". . . the hardest man I've ever met in my life. I got the impression that if you put a foot wrong, he would verbally tear you limb from limb, yet, at the same time, he commanded absolute loyalty through respect, not fear." Nor was he afraid of following his own judgement, even if it was contrary to the advice he was given.

Such an occasion arose early on. Edwardes had formed several groups of managers who had the task of examining the organisation of Leyland Cars and recommending a structure for the future. These cars organisation groups ("cogs") were assisted by the management consultancy, McKinsey. McKinsey and the cogs said the organisation should not be changed. Leyland Cars should continue to operate as a single entity.

Several executives disagreed with this view, among them Ray Horrocks, who had been recruited by Edwardes from the Eaton Corporation. Horrocks was a motor industry man, having worked for Ford from 1963 to 1972. He had then joined Eaton, but when Edwardes approached him was looking for a move because the company wanted him to go to work in the US. He became involved with BL during the closing weeks of 1977 and joined the company full time on January 1, 1978, although, at that time, he was not sure what he was going to do.

Horrocks took the view that the monolithic approach to BL would have made sense only if the monolith had been composed of companies that were viable. If that had been the case, some sharpening of relationships within those companies might have brought about the necessary improvement in performance. "But if they had been viable, we wouldn't have been there in the first place," he says. "I believed that the business should be divided, separated into its essential parts in order that we could look at the thing."

Edwardes agreed. His reasons, as explained in his book, were largely to do with the fact that "we had a classic case, on a massive scale, of faulty executive appointments – the wrong people in simply hundreds of key jobs . . ." Edwardes decided that the only way to tackle the difficulty was to change the organisation. "If that were done, new jobs would be created, old ones would disappear and every manager would have his suitability reassessed." His ideas on the future of Leyland Cars were diametrically opposed to those of Ryder. Where Ryder had believed in the Ford philosophy of one company embracing all of Leyland Cars' products, Edwardes took the view that the group was made up of different companies with widely differing needs.

Edwardes's explanations for his decision were peppered with phrases like the need to "get arms round trees", a reference to the supposedly unwieldy size of BL. But BL was small in terms of the world motor industry. Compared with Ford, General Motors or Toyota, it was tiny. Why, it might be asked, should its size be such an obstacle? Horrocks's explanation is that the companies with which BL was competing had grown by logical evolution. In the US, when takeovers had happened, the company taken over had been made to conform to the new parent's method of doing business. Those acquired by BL had been allowed to continue much as before. The Japanese car makers, on the other hand, had grown organically, without acquisitions.

The difficulties the company faced were far more complex than mere size would indicate. There was, to pick an example at random, the question of part numbers. Every component in a car has a part number. In the years since the formation of BLMC in 1968, some progress had been made on the use of common components. But at BL, a single component could have a multiplicity of numbers: for a factory, for movements between plants, for the market, for manuals. This caused confusion and there was always the risk that the company was failing to get the benefits of bulk ordering because separate orders were being placed for the same component. "This wasn't peculiar to BL," Horrocks says, "it was just more prevalent there."

On February 1, 1978, Edwardes announced that BL's cars operations would be split into three separate companies: Austin-Morris, Jaguar-Rover-Triumph (JRT) and BL Components. The theory was that each would be easier to manage because it was smaller. The decision was explained to the dealers at a meeting in the Wembley Conference Centre on February 3. It was here that Edwardes introduced the two men who were to run Austin-Morris and JRT: Ray Horrocks and Pratt Thompson. Pratt Thompson had been Deputy Managing Director of an electrical components company called Bowthorpe Holdings when Edwardes approached him to join BL. He had no experience of the motor industry, a fact that some people held against him. "In some respects, it took me longer to come to grips with key issues," Thompson admits. "On the other hand, it was an advantage because some people who said certain things couldn't be done because they'd never been done in the car industry were just plain wrong. Some basic things are common to any business."

The initial intention had been for Thompson to take on responsibility for BL Components, but Edwardes then offered him the post of chairman of JRT. For Thompson, that was a welcome development. The new division was seen as the "crown jewels" of BL. The formation of JRT and Austin-Morris was clearly a step in the right direction, but the decision to create BL Components would turn out to be one of the few fundamental mistakes that Edwardes and his board made. This division included several elements of the company that provided services to both Austin-Morris and JRT, including Unipart, the spare parts organisation, and Pressed Steel Fisher. Horrocks, while favouring reorganisation of the businesses, disagreed in part with the break-down decided on by Edwardes. "To expect someone to penetrate, at the top level, Leyland Cars in the short time that we had was incredible, simply because of the breadth of the businesses. I agreed with Michael on that, but I didn't agree with the way that he broke it down."

Horrocks believed that there should have been a volume car division including Austin, Morris and Rover. Jaguar would then have been joined with Triumph and Land Rover to create a specialist division. Land Rovers, however, were built in the same factory as Rover saloons. To put them in different divisions, it would have been necessary to divide the Rover factory at Solihull, with a separate management for each half. This was not thought to be a good idea and so Rover became a part of JRT. More important was the hiving-off of Pressed Steel Fisher, the body-building part of the company, into BL Components. That decision was to cause enormous difficulties within a short time.

Five days after the new structure was announced, Edwardes issued instructions that it should be completed by the end of April at the latest. Less than three months were allowed to decide how the new companies were to be staffed and operated. This was at a time when managers were under immense pressure to keep BL afloat from day to day. The reason for haste was that BL could not be allowed to appear to be without direction for too long.

The group was under close scrutiny by the press and Parliament.

A key element of Edwardes's decision was that the new organisation would enable the identities of the individual marques to be revived. JRT was conceived as a holding company. Each of the component parts had its own managing director. Of more interest to Jaguar, however, was the proposal that the group would have its own engineering department. Bob Knight, Jaguar's engineering director, was asked to go and see Edwardes in London. This was the first time Knight had met Edwardes and he experienced a characteristic of the new chairman's methods that was unnerving to some. "Although you were going to meet Michael Edwardes, you never knew how many other people would be present," he explains. There was an audience on this occasion, but Knight did not know the others present, and they were not introduced.

Edwardes explained his plan for a JRT engineering department, and offered Knight the job of running it. The appointment would, inevitably, have meant that Knight would have presided over the dismantling of the Jaguar engineering department that he had fought so hard to preserve. "I needed time to work out how to deal with this one, so I said, 'You'd expect me to take a day or so to think about how we'd run a Jaguar-Rover-Triumph engineering department.'" Knight also offered to provide his thoughts on the whole Jaguar-Rover-Triumph idea.

Edwardes had no objections but said he had to have Knight's response within four days and on no more than four pages. Knight met the deadline, just. He believes it was this paper that convinced Edwardes that he had found the right man to be Jaguar managing director. Knight was installed in the post early in 1978.

JRT became operational in July. It did not take long for Pratt Thompson to discover that he had been handed a troubled division. It had been assumed that Jaguar, along with Rover, Land Rover and Triumph made profits, although no one could prove it, because their figures were buried in the depths of BL's accounting systems. In the event, JRT made a profit before tax and interest of around £6 million during 1978. Thompson recalls that Land Rover made a significant profit, Jaguar broke even and Rover and Triumph between them lost around £40 million. That does not tally with the reconstructed figures later produced by John Edwards, who was to become Jaguar finance director in 1980, but however the figures worked out, the crown jewels began to look rather tarnished. Morale at Jaguar was at a low ebb. Rumours and uncertainties had affected everyone within the company. Bob Knight had managed to preserve the integrity of the engineering department and others had worked hard to keep Jaguar's individuality, but the years of fighting BL management had exacted a heavy toll.

Nor was the formation of JRT to prove the answer to their wishes. True, Jaguar had been re-formed as a company, and it had its own managing director again, but it was far from being autonomous. As Bob Knight puts it: "I was called managing director of an organisation that could neither buy anything nor sell anything." Many functions were run either by JRT or by central staffs. "All they did, really, was to create a Leyland Cars in miniature," Knight claims. He and his colleagues wanted real control of the company. That could not be achieved in the short term for two main reasons. First, some elements of the business had become too bound up with the totality of BL for them to be split out again quickly. Second, talented managers who knew Jaguar were in short supply. Recruitment was difficult, because few successful managers outside the company were prepared to join BL.

Thompson knew he had to convince Jaguar employees that he was prepared to fight for their future. The new AJ6 engine provided an unwelcome opportunity to do that. This engine was intended to replace the six-cylinder XK series in the saloon – code named XJ40 – that was being designed as a successor to the XJ6. Thompson says that gaining approval for it involved a battle with the BL board. "They wanted us to use the Rover V8 engine." That was both heresy to Jaguar people and, in Thompson's view, a marketing error. The Rover engine had originally been designed by General Motors for a medium-sized Buick saloon. In the mid-1960s, Rover had been trying to develop an engine to provide more power for the Rover 2000. William Martin-Hurst, at that time Rover managing director, had seen the V8 engine during a business trip to the US. A deal had been reached for Rover to make the engine under licence. The company carried out a considerable amount of development work on it before installing it in the Rover 3500 in 1968. Good though the engine was in Rover saloons and Range Rovers, Thompson and the Jaguar engineers were convinced that a lot more work would be needed to make it into the kind of refined power unit that was expected in a Jaguar. Even if that had been done, they thought using this engine involved large drawbacks.

Thompson pointed out to the BL board that a proportion of Jaguar customers bought the company's products because of the integrity of the design. "If we lose that percentage, you're further jeopardising this fragile animal called Jaguar," he told them. Perhaps more important would be the reaction of American customers. A high proportion of Jaguar sales were in the USA. "I would wager that at least half of those people are not going to be comfortable to know that they've got a Buick engine," Thompson said. "They're not going to spend $25,000 for a car that's got a General Motors V8." The argument raged for some time, some directors arguing that the engine could be changed cosmetically by fitting polished camshaft covers. It could also be further engineered, with four camshafts and by strengthening the bottom end. But that would take time that Jaguar did not have.

Bob Knight was called in to make presentations to the BL board. He recalls being warned that Ian MacGregor was a metallurgist and so expected a detailed, technical question from him. When the question came, Knight was able to answer it in depth and claims, as result, to have converted MacGregor, at least, to the Jaguar cause. Feelings about the suggestion that the Rover unit be used in a Jaguar still run high. Yet it was entirely reasonable for the BL board to raise the question. More concerned with the financial implications of the decision than with Jaguar's heritage, they were prepared to think the unthinkable and they did. A great deal of money would be needed to develop a new engine, and Jaguar was required to justify its assertion that that was necessary. Just as important, the AJ6 engine was noisy at that time. The design used an aluminium block, which is inherently less effective in suppressing noise than the more common cast iron. In addition, it had six cylinders, 24 valves and double overhead camshafts. There was, in the words of one executive, "a helluva lot happening at the top end". Jaguar engineers were to devote great efforts to achieving an acceptable degree of quietness. Before the argument was resolved, the Rover V8 was fitted by JRT engineers to XJ saloons and tested at the BL test track near Banbury, Oxfordshire. Word about these tests reached the engineering department at Jaguar, although no one there ever saw the cars. As one engineer put it, "They never came here. If they'd got through the gate, we'd have set fire to them."

Jaguar won the argument over the engine, but there was little that Thompson could do to satisfy its aspirations to complete independence. Jaguar still did not have control of the marketing effort overseas. That was dealt with through BL International. Nor did it have direct responsibility for sales in Britain. Thompson claims that part of the reason for this was the resistance of the dealers to yet another change. In the pre-Ryder days, dealers had to deal with Jaguar, Rover-Triumph and Austin-Morris separately. Each had its own sales force and its own sales administration. From the dealers' point of view, there were clear advantages in having one point of contact for all the models in what had been the Leyland Cars range. They also feared that they would eventually be asked to deal with Jaguar, Rover, Triumph, Land Rover and Austin-Morris as separate entities, and they resisted.

At the time, in 1978, the dealers were being courted by other manufacturers. Peugeot and Renault were flying BL dealers to their factories in France in attempts to get the better ones to defect. It was vital for BL to hang on to its dealers, and an ageing product range made the task no easier. In an effort to avoid alienating the dealers, a compromise was reached: a JRT sales team was set up. This was intended to be a short-term solution; plans were drawn up for a fully fledged sales and marketing department. In the meantime, Peter Murrough was appointed marketing director of JRT, and Alan Mazden sales operations manager.

The arrangement was far from ideal. Both JRT and Austin-Morris operated through the same dealer network, so both were competing for the time and attention of the same people. Bob Berry was, by this time, in charge of the Austin-Morris sales team. "Since we still operated through one network," he says, "we set out to make sure that the dominant factor continued to be the volume car division, partly through the pressure of the volumes that we had to sell, but partly through the setting up and running of a significant number of dealer-oriented promotions."

JRT also continued to draw on the expertise of Austin-Morris personnel in other areas, and was never a completely separate entity. That created frictions from the start. The question of staffing for JRT was a difficult one. The decisions on who would remain with Austin-Morris and who would go to JRT were made, for the most part, by the new Austin-Morris management. At the same time, several people were brought in from outside, some joining JRT from Leyland South Africa. Some were good; some, indeed, are still with Jaguar. There is no doubt, however, that some were inexperienced and a few were incompetent. None was a match for people in Austin-Morris who not only had a profound knowledge of the car industry, but were proven survivors. The sales and marketing people at JRT never stood a chance of winning ground among the dealer network when they faced opponents such as Bob Berry and Trevor Taylor, who were both now at Austin-Morris.

To strengthen the new JRT organisation, a corporate identity programme was developed. This was yet another issue that gave rise to arguments with central group staff. BL's logo and corporate colour (blue) were regarded as sacrosanct. There was a sizeable manual that dictated the ways in which the logo should be represented, and any manager who deviated from it was likely to be severely chastised. JRT wanted, not only to deviate, but to change the corporate colour from blue to green. Thompson maintains that there were good reasons for that. "We said that either the reorganisation was real or it wasn't," he recalls. "If it was real, then we needed to differentiate everything, from the product to the corporate identity of the company itself."

Eventually, a bright lime green was chosen, for reasons that are less than obvious. It is true that two of the companies within JRT had associations with green. Land Rover had always had a green logo and Jaguar could lay claim to British racing green. David Boole, now Jaguar's PR chief, was heavily involved. "One of the great sticking points was the presentation of dealer showrooms," he explains. "We were told British racing green would not work alongside blue. It was too dark. Nor would it work when backlit, illuminated fluorescently in signs." So JRT's corporate colour became lime green. In spite of the objections from BL staff, the new identity was adopted with the agreement of Michael Edwardes.

While these arguments were taking place, the major concern was still that cars were not selling fast enough. According to the registration figures issued by the Society of Motor Manufacturers and Traders, Jaguar's UK sales had been declining since 1974, when 14,493 cars had been sold. In 1977, the figure was only 9,387, and although 1978 was markedly better at 12,812, the slide was resumed in 1979, when sales totalled 8,035. Although the only figures available for export markets are Jaguar's own, and show deliveries rather than sales, the story was not much better abroad. The peak year for UK and export deliveries was 1971 when 32,589 cars were delivered. By 1977, that had fallen to 23,688. The figure rose again in 1978 to 27,346, but 1979 saw a steep decline to 14,861. The 1979 dip was not entirely unexpected. The Series III XJ6 and XJ12 models were introduced that March. Historically, Jaguar has always suffered a dip in sales while it brings its factories up to full operating levels after the changeover to a new model.

There was, however, an even bigger problem: the paint plant at Castle Bromwich, Birmingham. Thompson says this was almost the death of Jaguar. The company had not built its own bodies since the introduction of the smaller saloons in the mid-1950s. These had been the first Jaguars to use monocoque construction (without a chassis) and the bodies had been built by Pressed Steel at Castle Bromwich, which later built all Jaguar bodies. That reliance on Pressed Steel had been one of the factors that had persuaded Sir William Lyons to merge with the old BMC company. But there was a long standing desire at Jaguar that the company should have its own body shop and paint plant. It came close to being realised under Geoffrey Robinson, but the plans were aborted. So bodies continued to be built at Castle Bromwich and transported to Browns Lane for assembly. Jaguar people tended to believe that, if they were able to control the manufacture of bodies they would do it better than anyone else.

Some claim that this attitude led to a high level of rectification work on bodies arriving at Browns Lane. Charles Maple, director of quality for the cars group, is one who believes that Jaguar did more rectification work than was strictly necessary. There were strong arguments in favour of the body shop being on the same site as the design and assembly facilities. The XJ saloon was a prime example of what can happen where the two are separated. As Ray Horrocks puts it: "There was no awareness (at Jaguar) of the awful difficulties that a stylist can create for a guy trying to put together a body." In the case of the XJ saloon, this lack of awareness had resulted in styling lines at the front of the body which could not be achieved merely by pressing metal. The panels had to be pressed, welded or bolted together and then a team of men sculpted the lines using molten lead, a process known as lead loading. The shape was often further modified by filing the metal and as a result the paint shop was presented with bodies that had variable surfaces, consisting of a mix of steel and lead.

In the days when the bodies were painted with cellulose, this did not matter too much, since any marks that were on the bare body shell, known as the body in white, would be covered by the thickness of the paint. Then the final coat would be applied and polished, which gave a deep lustre to the finish. In 1978, however, a paint plant using a new technology, called thermoplastic acrylic (TPA) had been brought on stream. This was announced in the annual report for that year with the words: "Behind the high-gloss shine of the new Jaguar Series III models is an £18 million investment in the most advanced paint shop in Britain."

The reality was that, although the new facility achieved a high gloss finish, this merely served to highlight the deficiencies of the body underneath. Mike Beasley, today Jaguar's assistant managing director, explains that TPA is a form of Perspex. When applied as a paint, it looks dull; the body is then put into an oven, and the TPA melts and re-flows over the surface. Unfortunately, the thinness of the paint layer and its high gloss created problems. "If you imagine stretching cling film over something," Beasley says, "you'd see every imperfection underneath by virtue of the reflection. That's exactly what you got with TPA." Difficulties multiplied. The temperature at which the paint flowed was close to that at which the lead loading melted, so the paint was flowing across a soft surface on parts of the body. Once the paint had been heated, it could not be polished; and it was brittle and chipped easily.

All of which prompts the question, why was TPA used in the first place? No one seems able to answer it satisfactorily. It had been recommended by General Motors in America, although Ray Horrocks claims that GM was replacing it even before it had been installed at Castle Bromwich. But paint technology was not the only problem at Castle Bromwich. Ken Edwards was at that time responsible for ensuring that deadlines on new product development were met. He says the 126 motors that powered the track were not strong enough to take all the bodies. Beasley points out that some of the men operating the equipment were poorly trained.

So the new plant used the wrong technology, in an inadequate facility with insufficient training for the operators. Jaguar felt that it had cause for complaint. But PSF claimed that the high rate of rejection of painted bodies delivered to Browns Lane was unreasonable. Arguments began about who was responsible. The PSF inspectors were adamant that the bodies were good when they left the paint plant. The Jaguar inspectors were just as adamant that they were unusable when they arrived at Browns Lane. There was something approaching open warfare between the two camps. Jaguar went so far as to begin searching for other suppliers to paint the bodies, and even had discussions with Opel in Germany, according to Thompson. "Can you imagine, transporting bodies across Europe?" he asks. "That's how desperate the situation was."

Eventually, Thompson had a private meeting with Michael Edwardes and told him that either the paint plant came under Jaguar's control or he wanted to be formally relieved of responsibility for Jaguar. "I didn't want the disappearance of Jaguar to be down to me," he says, "and that is what would have happened." Edwardes's solution was to call Charles Maple to London and give him the task of overcoming the difficulty. Maple became a mediator between Jaguar and Pressed Steel Fisher and the experience seems to have left scars. Even today, Maple is reluctant to talk about this period. Three men were involved: Maple himself, David Fielden from Jaguar and Andrew Barr, who had been brought in to run PSF. Their task was to establish acceptable quality standards. Maple says he tried to make filing of bodies a cardinal sin and that, between them, they tried to find an alternative to lead for the final sculpting of styling lines.

In due course, some of the trouble caused by faults in the body in white was overcome by baking the paint at a lower temperature. When faults were highlighted by the paint, they could be rectified and the paint cut and polished in the traditional fashion. That meant that some parts of the body, such as the areas inside the door apertures, were not as glossy as they would have been had the TPA process been followed. However, this was seen as an acceptable consequence of achieving a better standard of finish on the more visible areas of the body.

For Horrocks, the overall goal was clear. He wanted Jaguar to have control of that part of the Castle Bromwich plant that built Jaguar bodies, but he was equally firm in his conviction that it had to be turned into an effective body building plant first. It took until the middle of 1980 before any real progress was made towards that goal. The paint was merely the worst of the quality problems at Jaguar that were alienating increasing numbers of owners. Thompson had first-hand experience of the annoyance caused by faults that were often small in themselves. Soon after being appointed chairman, he was allocated a green XJ12 saloon. This had been a demonstrator for use by the press, so it had been meticulously maintained. On three separate occasions, he left his home at 4.30 a.m. to go to work only to find that the car would not start. The fault was finally traced to the switch that operated the boot light. It was not being operated when the boot was shut and the light drained the battery. Horrocks was another victim. "I had three Jaguars, one after the other, and they were absolutely miserable," he recalls. "In the end, I learnt how to leap out of the car when it wouldn't start and whip off the fuel enrichment device, put two thumbs over the spout and fire her up again. I learnt all the tricks that you had to know."

The cars were plagued with electrical faults, but there were arguments between Jaguar and their main electrical equipment supplier, Lucas, as to the source of these faults. Shortcomings existed on both sides. Jaguar's specifications were defective in some instances; in others, the quality of the components was suspect. Maple introduced a system of encouraging suppliers to tell designers that they would not make a component either to the specification, or for use in the position, that the designers wanted if they believed that what was being demanded was wrong. He admits that it was difficult to gain acceptance for the system. "It takes a lot of nerve for a supplier to say 'I won't do that', when there's a risk that the manufacturer will go to someone else who will," he says.

But it was too late in many cases. Components had been designed and made that did not do their jobs. Lucas and Dunlop put small teams into America to provide feedback to directors and senior managers on electrical and tyre defects. One of the men in the Lucas team maintains that Jaguar itself was responsible for much of the trouble. He says the electrical system was not powerful enough for all the equipment fitted. Jaguar engineers had not, for instance, foreseen that a car might be driven considerable distances with the air conditioning running full blast at the same time as both headlights and wipers were in use. Yet the conditions that required so much equipment were fairly commonplace in some states. Jaguar's response is that it had to buy many components off the shelf, rather than have them specifically designed, and there were no readily available alternators that could deliver enough power.

The Lucas man also claims that a decision taken at Jaguar reduced the reliability of the fuel injection system on the XJ12. Ironically, that decision had been taken in an attempt to improve reliability. The amplifier that controlled the injection system was mounted between the two banks of cylinders on the V12 engine. This was to enable the engine to be tested with its own electronics fitted before being installed in the body, instead of being linked to a slave unit for testing. Unfortunately, the area between the cylinders is hostile for electronics. The temperature variations are enormous and this caused frequent failure of the equipment.

Extensive programmes were introduced to try to eliminate these and other faults, but it was a long job that tied up scarce engineering resources. Work was already well in hand on the successor to the XJ6 saloon. This was more than usually demanding because the company was mesmerised by the need to achieve high fuel efficiency, particularly for the American market. The engineers were attempting to squeeze around 27 miles per gallon out of the new car; that meant making it a lot lighter. That was a major task in itself, and at the same time, the company was trying to make the Series III XJ6 and XJ12 reliable.

In the midst of all these difficulties, arguments developed about the location of the planned JRT sales and marketing team. Cedric Scroggs was convinced that the marketing people should be at Browns Lane, close to the engineering and manufacturing staffs, to make possible a rapid exchange of information. But Browns Lane was already full to bursting. Thompson wanted all Jaguar managers to be at the factory, to give the new organisation a feeling of being a complete team. So the new marketing director was installed at Browns Lane, but there was no room for his staff, who were installed in Leyland's old Coventry House building in the centre of Coventry.

By the late summer of 1979, it was becoming clear that the basis on which the divisions had been formed was fundamentally flawed. The belief had been that Austin-Morris was in the worst trouble and that splitting it off from JRT would allow Horrocks and his team to concentrate on sorting it out. But circumstances had overtaken the planning. It was now clear that, of the companies that made up JRT, one was unlikely to last much longer. Triumph had been making a large saloon, the 2000, but that had been superseded by the new Rover 3500. The Dolomite range was old and there were no plans for a replacement since the SD2, which would have been the new, small product from JRT, had been cancelled owing to lack of money. The TR7 was in doubt because of the problems of modifying the engine to meet the exhaust emissions requirements in America, its biggest market. But there had been huge investment in the Rover plant at Solihull, so Triumph was doomed.

The board, possibly with the encouragement of the new Conservative government, was thinking of the future, too. In the long term, the intention was to return BL to the private sector, and it was felt that this would have to be done piecemeal. Land Rover had seemed likely to be the first candidate for privatisation, but the collapse of its main African markets meant that it would need supporting for much longer than had been expected. Jaguar was next in line, but the pre-condition for floating it off was that it had to be made into a self-contained car manufacturer, so far as that was possible.

Edwardes concluded that the structure had to be changed yet again, and he asked Horrocks to take on the job of managing a merged Austin-Morris/Rover-Triumph operation. Pratt Thompson moved across to run BL International and Percy Plant was installed at Browns Lane to keep things running while a new man was found for the top job at Jaguar. That caused concern at Jaguar, because Plant had built his reputation closing factories. Horrocks says: "If Percy Plant arrived, your days were numbered. This was the harbinger of closing down because he'd done a lot of that. He was very good at it." Yet there was no intention of closing Jaguar. It was simply that Plant was the only senior man available to take over.

The changes were described in the 1979 annual report as "streamlining" and, in October of that year, a new sales and

Sir John Egan, architect of Jaguar's recovery since 1980.

Sir William Lyons, founder of Jaguar, who ran the company until his retirement in 1972.

Geoffrey Robinson Chief Executive of Jaguar from 1973 to 1975.

Bob Knight who did so much to retain Jaguar Engineering Department as a separate entity.

Le Mans 1988 and the race winning Jaguar XJR9 driven by Jan Lammers, Johnny Dumfries and Andy Wallace. *(Motor Sport.)*

One of the racing XJ5.3 coupes at Silverstone in 1977 shortly after the decision had been taken to disband the team. *(Motor Sport.)*

The start of the 1956 Le Mans 24 hour race. Car numbers 1, 2 and 3 were the last Jaguars to be entered in the race by the factory. Car number 4, entered by the Scottish Team, Ecurie Ecosse, went on to win. *(Motor Sport.)*

Goldrush, the offshore racing boat powered by twin turbocharged Jaguar V12 engines that raced in 1984.

The old paint shop at the Jaguar factory at Browns Lane. Plans to replace it foundered when BLMC ran out of money in 1974.

Building XJ6 saloons in the early nineteen seventies, on the cramped final assembly lines at Browns Lane.

Jaguar XJ40 assembly at an early stage. Body panels are covered with bubble plastic to protect them.

The 'body drop'. An XJ40 body is mated with engine, transmission and rear axle assemblies in one movement on the assembly line at Browns Lane.

Potential customers assess the XJ40 at a styling clinic. This is a full-size model of the car with no engine and no interior trim.

A prototype XJ40 on test in Australia some months before public launch.

emonstrating the role of Body Engineering at one of the J Days organised at the
ational Exhibition Centre for Jaguar employees and their families.

aguar XJ40s lined up ready to be tested by American journalists at the press
unch at Tucson, Arizona in March 1987.

The London Motor Show at Earls Court, 1968. Attention is centred on the new Jaguar XJ6, on show in Britain for the first time. *(Topham Picture Library.)*

The British Motor Show at the National Exhibition Centre, Birmingham in 1986. The new XJ40 on display, ten days after being announced.

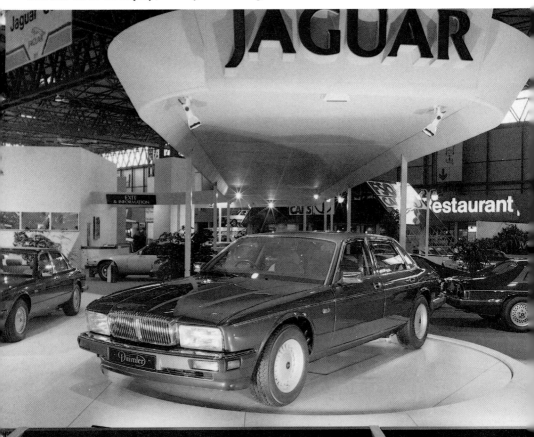

marketing organisation was set up for all the car companies. It was called BL Europe and Overseas (BLEO) and Tony Ball was installed as chairman. At a conference for dealers held at the Wembley Conference Centre on September 13, 1979, Edwardes explained why the new organisation had been created. In doing this, he referred to a meeting that had been held 16 months before. "There was a lot of pressure from your representatives at the top, the people whom we dealt with at the time . . . for a single, strong, sales and marketing organisation. With hindsight, I think they were right and we are, in fact, doing it."

Austin, Morris, Rover and Triumph were now in one organisation known as Light Medium Cars; Land Rover, Jaguar and Unipart were all separate; BLEO acted for all the car companies while Land Rover had a separate sales and marketing team. All of these new groupings reported to Ray Horrocks, who became chairman of a new holding company called BL Cars. BLEO was an unwelcome development at Jaguar. They had begun to move towards having their own sales and marketing organisation again, only to have the prospect snatched away from them. They expected little sympathy from the new management because Tony Ball had been an Austin-Morris man in the past and his managing director was Trevor Taylor, who had been with the volume cars side of the business for several years.

Ball had been in the motor industry since leaving school. He had begun as an apprentice at Austin, and had risen through the ranks to become its youngest ever sales manager. His family had been Austin and Morris dealers in the West Country for 40 years and he had been chairman of the cars distribution side of Barlow Handling, with 19 dealers under him. Several of them had been Jaguar dealers. He had also run a Ford dealership in South Africa. His qualifications were impressive, and he had a deep seated belief in the need for a British motor manufacturer. He recalls that the reasons for setting up BLEO went beyond the dealers' desire to have one sales and marketing organisation. "We were reducing the headcounts by 90,000 at that stage in the game, so it wasn't appropriate to set up an independent sales force and marketing organisation for Jaguar in isolation," he says. BLEO was set up for two reasons: to meet dealers' demands and to avoid duplication of staffs.

One of the major tasks of the new organisation was to retain as many dealers as possible. This was far from easy. Dealers in the UK and America had become disenchanted with the franchises. Many of them were attracted by other manufacturers and the rate of defections had reached alarming proportions. BLEO was very much a holding operation, and part of the objective in setting up was to allow Jaguar to put its manufacturing house in order. Once that had been done, it could assume responsibility for sales and marketing and would take one more step to being an independent car manufacturer. Since Plant was no more than a caretaker, a new managing director had to be found. Horrocks began searching for one.

Many believe that Jaguar-Rover-Triumph was a failure, because it was disbanded after so short a time. For Jaguar, it did, at least, bring the benefit that the company was soon (in mid-1980) to gain control of the body plant. Although the company now entered a period of limbo, it was a step closer to autonomy.

CHAPTER 4
The Arrival of Egan

Several people were considered for the job of Jaguar managing director; one of them was John Egan. He had been approached by BL in 1977 and asked to run Jaguar-Rover-Triumph. Egan turned the offer down because, he says, he did not believe Edwardes understood the magnitude of BL's troubles. "I felt that Michael Edwardes was being unrealistic when he started, as to how much of the company could be saved," he says.

However, now that Jaguar was to be separated, things were different. Horrocks discussed with Edwardes the possibility of approaching Egan again. They decided that they had nothing to lose by trying to persuade him to take over at Jaguar. Egan was invited to a meeting late in 1979, and it transpired that his career with Massey Ferguson was at a turning point. He spent most of his time in Europe, although his job was supposed to be in Toronto. "I had a big question mark," he explains. "Was I going to remain working abroad, or was I going to come back to the UK again?" This time, he saw reason to consider Edwardes's offer more seriously.

First, he had seen how Edwardes had begun to tackle some of BL's difficulties. "I thought that he was certainly tackling the industrial relations area with far more ferocity and seriousness than anybody else had," he says. Second, the Conservatives had been voted into office in 1979 and this led Egan to think that there was "a far more realistic view being taken of the country at large". Third, the Conservatives were committed to reducing the highest levels of personal taxation. "I certainly felt as though working in the UK might be a realistic proposition," comments Egan. In April, 1980, Egan took over as managing director of Jaguar Cars Holdings, in which all the Jaguar companies had been grouped at the beginning of the year.

Born in 1940, Egan had been involved in the motor industry for much of his working life. After gaining a BSc at Imperial College, London, he had joined Shell as a petroleum engineer, and stayed until 1966. While with Shell, he noticed that engineers tend to be poor business managers, so he set about rectifying the shortcoming in himself by spending two years gaining a master's degree at the London Business School. This experience appears to have influenced his approach to management training when he joined Jaguar. He became general manager with General Motors' AC Delco Replacement Parts business in Britain before joining BL for the first time in 1971. There, he was instrumental in setting up Unipart, the group's parts operation. In 1976, he joined Massey Ferguson and by the time he talked to Edwardes and Horrocks, he was corporate parts director of the company's construction and machinery division.

He has been decribed as a "blunt Lancastrian"; his instinct is to go straight to the heart of any problem. In a magazine interview he said: "I like to get the whole problem up front. I'm certainly the least devious person you'll ever meet and I try to make sure the facts are well established and that people are basing their actions and their understanding of the situation on facts." He is said by his managers to be good at delegating. As one puts it: "He gets involved up to the neck in everything that you want him to and gives you total support, but once he realises that he no longer has to do that . . . he moves on to something else." Egan has gained widespread respect and admiration both within the company and outside. His appointment was probably one of the most inspired actions taken within BL.

Egan joined BL as managing director of Jaguar Cars Holdings (with Horrocks as his chairman) and as chairman of Jaguar Cars Ltd, which owned the manufacturing plant at Browns Lane and the engine factory at Radford, in Coventry. From the very beginning, Egan made two things abundantly clear: he believed that Jaguar should be totally autonomous; and he was in complete control. The question of independence for the company brought him into conflict with several people, not least Horrocks and Ball. Egan took the view that, to be autonomous, Jaguar had to have control of the whole business, from building and painting the bodies to sales and marketing.

Horrocks did not budge from his belief that the body shop and the paint plant had to be put right before being handed over to Jaguar. "The essence was to get the paint plant right, on site, largely by the guys who put the thing in," he says. Progress was aready being made when Egan arrived, but it was to take several months before he was given control of body in white and paint. This was the first time in its history that Jaguar was to have control of almost all of the manufacturing process. But it still did not run everything. Pressing of the panels used to build the bodies was to remain outside the company for several years.

While Egan gained control of the body plant fairly quickly, the view within BL was that he and his team had enough to do improving manufacturing quality without trying to tackle the sales and marketing difficulties at the same time. So BLEO continued to provide those services. This also avoided duplication of effort. Jaguars were sold through the same network as the volume cars, and it was felt that setting up a separate sales team was a luxury the company could not afford. The financial problems were so severe that Egan was told, from the outset, that he had to begin turning the company around. If he could not make progress, Jaguar would be closed. "I certainly appreciated that if the thing wasn't showing signs of recovery, it'd be closed down," he says. "I was under absolutely no illusion that we were indispensable."

Closure of Jaguar would no doubt have caused a public uproar, but the BL board was not overconcerned about that. It had, after all, weathered the storm caused by closing MG. Viewed dispassionately, the ultimatum was understandable. In 1980, Jaguar made a pre-tax loss of £47.3 million. Only 15,469 cars were sold – the lowest level for more than 20 years; 13,791 cars were produced by 9,210 employees – less than 1.5 cars per employee. In America, the opinion research company, J. D. Power, produced horrifying statistics. According to J. D. Power, only 20 per cent of Jaguar's American customers were satisfied with their cars 35 days after taking delivery. John Edwards, who joined the company as finance director in July 1980, found that the financial position was much worse than anyone expected. "In 1980," he says, "we'd have gone out of business if we'd been a separate company, on our own, funding ourselves."

Apart from low production rates, and poor quality, the company faced severe external difficulties. When Egan joined, inflation stood at just under 22 per cent and the price of petrol had risen for the fifth time in just under a year. In April 1979, a gallon of four star had cost 84 pence. By April 1980 it had risen to 134 pence. This was bad news for a company that made thirsty cars like the XJ12, but worse was to come. America was Jaguar's most important single export market. If events moved against the company there, the chances of bringing about any real improvement in financial performance were severely damaged. That is exactly what happened in 1980.

The world was losing confidence in the US. The seizure of hostages in the American embassy in Tehran and President Carter's stance over the invasion of Afghanistan by the USSR contributed to this loss of confidence. As a result, sterling rose in value against the dollar. In January, a pound had been worth 2.27 dollars. By September, it had hit 2.40 dollars. A car that had sold for $25,000 in 1979 had brought the company £13,000; the same car sold at the same price when the dollar hit its low in 1980 brought in only £10,400. It is, perhaps, fortunate, that only about 3,000 Jaguars were sold in America in 1980, although the company began offering discounts to dealers of up to $4,000 (about £1,800) off the price of each XJ12 and XJ-S. This was to clear unsold stocks of 1979 model year cars. After the high in September, the pound fell a little but then rose to $2.40 in January 1981. After that, confidence returned to the dollar and by the following August, th pound was worth only $1.82.

It was ollar movements as much as anything that saved the compar from closure. The rise in the value of the dollar brought the company a welcome cash windfall and a breathing space to allow it to make the many improvements that were needed. In March 1981, the BL board met to discuss the possible closure of the Rover factory at Solihull, and of Browns Lane. It decided to shut Solihull and shift production of the SD1 Rover to Cowley.

A decision on Browns Lane (closure of which could have meant transferring Jaguar production to another BL plant, possibly Longbridge) was deferred, to give the new management a chance to turn the business round. As John Edwards puts it: "We got, if you like, an amber light to stay alive."

While these difficulties were waiting for Egan in the future, he walked into Jaguar in the midst of a far more immediate crisis. The assembly workers were on strike and no cars were being built at Browns Lane. The strike had its roots in the recovery plan that had been put together by Edwardes and his team, and that appeared in September 1979. One of the main aims of the plan was to restore to managers the responsibility for managing. For years, they had been unable to do anything without the agreement of the unions. Edwardes wanted to bring that situation to an end and, at the same time, increase labour mobility in the factories. The plan was set out in a comprehensive document that was discussed with the unions at national level over several months. These discussions also included the annual pay award and revisions to the grading structure. It was this that caused the most friction at Jaguar.

The proposal was that unskilled employees would receive a 5 per cent pay increase and skilled employees 10 per cent. The aim was to restore differentials, and to try to stop the flow of craftsmen who were leaving BL. At the same time, a new grading system was to be introduced. As part of this system, the assembly workers at Jaguar were to be regraded and, in their eyes, de-moted. They had always regarded themselves as superior to men working on the tracks in other factories. They were building a more complex car, a luxury product, and so, according to their logic, they must be more skilled than men building Minis at Longbridge. Horrocks admits that there was some truth in this. "There was a higher skill required. It's also true that, whereas an assembly line worker was usually grade 3 and a skilled worker grade 2 and craftsman such as a toolmaker grade 1, the mix of 2s in the Jaguar plant was richer than in any other place."

Matters came to a head just before Easter, 1980. By this time, discussions had been going on for five months, and Edwardes decided to force a conclusion. He told the unions that anyone who reported for work after Easter would be assumed to have accepted the pay and conditions package. The justification for this was that the employees had voted in a postal ballot over-whelmingly in favour of the recovery plan, which included the principles that were now being debated with the shop stewards. Therefore, according to Edwardes, the only point at issue was the detail and more than enough time had been spent discussing that without any result. Most employees agreed that there should be no strike over this issue, but at Browns Lane, it was claimed by some shop stewards that 1,500 assembly workers stayed away from work. Within days, the Jaguar men had been joined in their strike by others from the factories building Land Rovers, Range Rovers and Sherpa vans, who had similar grievances. On Friday, April 11, the Transport and General Workers' Union, which represented the assembly workers, declared the strike official throughout the group. To some extent, the strike became a battle between the TGWU and the Amalgamated Union of Engineering Workers. The AUEW, which represented a high proportion of skilled men, told its members to work normally. The TGWU wanted an all-out stoppage.

On April 16, Edwardes issued an ultimatum. Unless the TGWU members returned to work by April 23, all 18,500 of them would be sacked. The following day, Moss Evans of the TGWU led his negotiating team into a negotiating session that was to last nine hours. He finally agreed to terms that were little different from those that had triggered the strike. On April 22, the strikers went back to work, except at Jaguar. They met the next day and decided to stay out, even though the company had offered an appeals panel to discuss the grading issue. Union representatives met senior managers over the weekend of April 24–25 to try to thrash out an agreement that would bring the dispute to an end. Egan had taken up his new job only 10 days before this meeting and explains that he was advised by some BL people that the strike was nothing to do with him and therefore, he could stand aloof from it. He did not accept the advice. "My estimation of the situation was that if something wasn't done, Jaguar would get closed down and that would be the end of that," he says. "I remember saying to myself that I might easily be the only chairman of a car company never to make a car."

The fact that Egan was new to the company gave him an advantage when he began negotiating with the union leaders that weekend. He could, in effect, promise a fresh start. At the same time, it meant that the union people would have to take a great deal on trust. "All I could say was, well, here's my brief, to do the best I can for the company," says Egan. "We'll put together the bits and pieces of it. The decision-making of most of the company will be here, right in front of you and we'll do our very best. It's the only chance you've got. If you chuck up this chance, well that's it, you can forget about it all."

After 16 hours of talks on the Sunday, the unions agreed to recommend an end to the strike, on the basis of Egan's promise to "do the right thing by the men". The management's terms were unchanged. The following day, the men voted, by a narrow majority, to return to work. That was only the first of a succession of hurdles facing Egan. Another was Bob Knight. Knight had been managing director of Jaguar during the JRT days, but Egan had been brought in specifically to do that job. Egan apparently tried to persuade Knight to stay, but he chose to take early retirement instead.

During those early months, Egan set about establishing what had to be done to save the company. Apart from the obvious need to improve quality, the dealer network had to be overhauled. Too many dealers were not selling enough cars and not making enough profit out of the franchise. There was little that Egan could do about this, because he did not control his sales and marketing, nor did he control franchising policy. All of that was the responsibility of BLEO, which had set up a separate section to look after Jaguar sales and marketing. On the sales side, Bob Berry once again became involved with the company. The initial intention was for Berry to act as a link between Jaguar and BLEO. The concept changed quickly, however. "In the reorganisation under Tony Ball," Berry explains, "it was decided to set up a Jaguar area with half a dozen people. I ran that." Berry maintains that Ball was strongly in favour of a separate Jaguar team. So was Bert Lawrence, who was responsible for Far Eastern markets. Berry's small team was based in BL's sales and marketing building at Bickenhill, between Birmingham and Coventry.

For Egan, this was always an unacceptable state of affairs. He wanted control of the sales and marketing of his products and he took every opportunity to try to get it. He says the main sticking point was the question of sales forecasts. He was convinced that Jaguar could sell more cars than the BLEO forecasters thought possible. The result was an acrimonious relationship between Egan and Ball. Indeed, Ball was driven to complain to Horrocks on one occasion that the experience was "legalised mugging". Horrock's reaction was to tell Ball that he was "standing up very well to it", which suggests that he was less than sympathetic. But Horrocks was well aware of the pressures on Ball. "He had a helluva job to do with a very wide assignment. He was launching a new product virtually every year. . . . It was a very complex organisation too, and of course, the manufacturing people were absolutely convinced that they could do a better job (than BLEO)." Horrocks adds, "John Egan certainly believed he could sell cars better than Tony."

Berry also defends Ball. "He was under enormous pressure to make sure that this fledgling organisation toed the line. He steered a very difficullt course . . . recognising that a potentially irresistible force was building up in Browns Lane under John Egan and he'd better be seen to be a part of it." Berry was caught in the crossfire, employed by one of the warring factions, but expected to provide ammunition for the other to attack his own organisation. Egan never missed an opportunity to berate the BLEO directors, and stories still circulate of the way he would pound the table and say that he would not pay the BLEO people in washers. After 18 months, Berry decided that enough was enough, and left.

During the summer of 1981, the American dealers were brought to Coventry in an attempt to convince them that the company had a future. At the time, Egan was having to make monthly reports to the BL board which was still ready to pull the plug if it had to.

Today, Egan admits that he did not realise how close Jaguar came to being closed down. The BL board had approved the funds needed for the development of XJ40, the new saloon, apparently on the basis that it could be built at Longbridge if Browns Lane were closed. However, the government then had to approve the board's decision. Egan comments: "I now know that there was a heck of a struggle to get the money, in which Norman Tebbit had to work very hard with Keith Joseph . . . to persuade the Prime Minister to give us the money. We were under close examination."

Part of that examination involved acceptance of the company's 1982 budget. The budget, in turn, depended on sales forecasts and here again Egan was at loggerheads with BLEO. The discussion took place mid-way through 1981, and the key to it was the US. "We'd sold 3,000 cars in 1980 and every year had been getting smaller and smaller," explains Egan. "We'd no idea what was going to happen in '81. As it turned out, it was 4,700. BLEO saw that as some minor aberration. They were forecasting 2,500 for '82 and wouldn't shift from that, simply wouldn't shift." In the end Egan wore them down and they did shift substantially, accepting a forecast of 6,000 cars for the US, but then others had to be persuaded. The American dealers were to have a dinner at a Stratford hotel, Egan and Ball were to address them afterwards.

Egan told the dealers that after they had left the factory that day, he had spoken to some of the workforce, who had wanted to know what the Americans had thought of the 1982 model year car that they had seen. He said that he had told them it was difficult to say, but that the Americans' sales forecast for the following year was so low there would be few cars to make anyway. This was a ploy to get the American dealers to back the 6,000 target he had forced through BLEO. The US dealer council had already discussed it, but had not yet committed itself to it. If it refused to do so, Egan knew he would be in severe difficulties.

Egan recalls: "Robbie Robinson, who was vice-president of the dealer council, stood up and said, 'I think I'm speaking on behalf of all the southern California dealers. We can make the 6,000 sales forecast.' Then somebody else stood up and said, 'I speak for the State of New York, and we can . . .' and then there was all kinds of shouting and just as they were saying, 'Yes, go for it, go for the 6,000,' we brought the Band of the Grenadier Guards in," says Egan. "There was this great big banging and noise, and everybody shouting, '6,000, 6,000', and so that was how we settled our sales forecast for 1982." One of the purposes of bringing the Americans to Britain was to show them the new cars for 1982 and, in particular, the new XJ12 and XJ-S with the newly developed high efficiency (HE) cylinder heads. David Boole, now Jaguar's director of communications and public affairs, suggested that the launch of the revised XJ-S should be presented to the press as a major event. "Although a new engine is not the greatest news in the world," he explains, "it was the only thing that Jaguar had to say for itself in terms of major product changes for a long time. I said that here was an opportunity to generate a lot of interest in Jaguar cars which wouldn't repeat itself for some time."

There is no doubt that the improved XJ-S desperately needed the best launch that could be devised. The car had been selling so badly that production had been stopped and there had been serious discussion about discontinuing it. In 1981, 1,252 were delivered to dealers. Boole comments: "The advice that BLEO marketing were giving to John (Egan) at that stage was, 'It's not worth carrying on with the XJ-S. You ought to can it and just concentrate on the saloon.'"

The HE head improved fuel consumption from about 11 miles per gallon to about 15, and Peter Battam, who was handling advertising for Jaguar at BLEO, has no doubts about its importance for the XJ-S. "It made V12 and 5 litres respectable and the S took off," he says. After the introduction of the new engine and other changes that were made to the car's specification, sales took off to such an extent that Egan was quoted in 1985 as saying: "The XJ-S is doing very well. We'll build nearly 8,000 of them this year and we'll make a damn sight more money out of them than we did from the 13,000 saloons we made in 1980."

Not only did the company improve the specifications of its 1982 model year cars, it rationalised its pricing. Over the preceding years, BL had tended to "load" the prices, and the opportunity was taken to correct that. The prices of most models were reduced, by up to 9.5 per cent. The average price cut was 3.2 per cent. By the end of 1981, the company was back in profit on a month-by-month basis, and the pressure had eased. Egan was allowed to begin building up his own sales and marketing department. In December, he was attending the dealer launch of the Austin Ambassador and the revised Rover saloons. Neil Johnson was also present as director, continental Europe, for BLEO. Johnson had been around BL for many years and so already knew Egan. He asked him how things were going. "Terrific, except I need a sales and marketing director," Egan replied. "Are you interested?" Johnson was very interested. "I'd always felt that there was a bigger market potential for Jaguar," he explains. "The managing directors of the individual sales companies (in the European markets) were in the business of the art of the possible, and if they were being pressurised to sell 15,000 Metros and 6,000 Allegros or whatever it might have been, then the 300 or 400, or sometimes even fewer, Jaguars in their portfolios took less than their full attention."

To overcome that difficulty, Johnson had begun to set up separate sales organisations for Jaguar and Land Rover. "I was concerned that we shouldn't drop out of the specialist market out of neglect." His knowledge of the specialist car market was useful, but Johnson also knew the extent of Jaguar's quality problems as a result of time spent in the service division. Even so, it was a gesture of faith on Johnson's part to take the sales and marketing director's job. There was no confidence within BLEO that Jaguar could survive. Anyone who wanted the safe route would have chosen to stay with BLEO. Fortunately for Jaguar, several talented people decided to take the risk and go with Johnson, who set up his own team as soon as his appointment was confirmed.

He moved into Browns Lane in the spring of 1982.

Shortly before, he had appeared at a BL Cars dealer council meeting at Stratford. The dealer council is the negotiating body that handles policy matters arising between dealers and the company. It is a potent lobbying force and has occasionally savaged senior managers with whom it was dissatisfied. One insider recalls with some bitterness: "If they wanted to kill a programme, they killed a programme. If they wanted to have an individual, they had an individual. They were very powerful."

Johnson was introduced as Jaguar's sales and marketing director elect, and he outlined his strategy for the franchise. "That was to rip through the dealer network in the UK," he explains, "to rid the network of the Jaguar dealers in name only . . . and then set about the standards of the others." Reaction was mixed. Johnson says comments during the lunch break were almost evenly divided between those who thought the plan was madness and those who thought it was what was needed. He quickly found an ally when he appointed Roger Putnam as UK sales operations director. Putnam had been working for Lotus, and had watched how Porsche developed their UK dealer network. "They had only 29 dealers selling about 100 cars per outlet," he recalls. "When I came on board, we (Jaguar) had nearly 300 dealers selling 18 cars per outlet per year."

Some time later, there was a dealer conference at the factory. Johnson spoke again, and this time, he put forward specific proposals. "I said, I believed that in 12 or 18 months' time, we would be down to 150 dealers and that we would probably go below that." The message must have been received with mixed emotions by some dealers. They faced a fifty-fifty chance of losing the franchise. Yet, as Johnson explained, the process was intended to attack the company's tarnished image. Discounts of £1,000 were commonly being offered on Jaguars, and dealers were poaching customers from each other's territory in an attempt to achieve the sales levels they needed to survive. Standards of service were appalling and the product was in danger of losing its luxury cachet. Egan recalls stories he heard about some of the dealers, ". . . companies with no demonstrators, companies unwilling to demonstrate a car, companies who were insisting customers put petrol in so that they could have a demonstration. It was a nightmare. We were selling cars in spite of some dealers." Egan is quick to point out that others were doing a good job. But they all had to improve.

Putnam explains the thinking behind the move to reduce the numbers of dealers: "I believed you sold more cars by appointing fewer dealers, more specialist dealers than by following the normal volume car philosophy of appointing more dealers to sell more cars." He was absolutely opposed to the idea of using Jaguars and Daimlers as bait for the dealers, to try to improve sales of the volume car marques. But this was to be much more than a refinement of the dealer network. What was being proposed, and soon implemented, was a redefinition of the company's franchising needs. No dealer was to be regarded as indispensable.

It was clear that the job had to be finished before XJ40 was launched. "Unless we got our franchising correct by the time we launched XJ40, we would go through what Jaguar had been through many times before, which was an enormous upsurge when 40 was launched and then the inevitable trough afterwards," says Putnam. The process began by analysing car registration information by postal code in order to define the main markets for Jaguars and Daimlers. Each geographical market area had to provide the potential for 25 new car sales per dealer per year. Putnam maintains that it was too much to expect a dealer who had been selling fewer than 18 cars a year to make the step to 25. "So we decided anybody who was selling less than 25 went. Some of the others were of such an appalling standard they went as well. The first 70 or 80 terminations were very simple. They were expecting it."

Having taken the first steps in firing sub-standard dealers, Jaguar turned its attention to the main urban areas. "My comment was that there was no point worrying about the fens if you hadn't got London, Birmingham, Manchester franchised properly, because you're talking about 80 per cent of your volume potentially," Putnam says. A series of market areas was mapped that would each provide a viable business for one dealer. Those territories were then laid over the map showing where there were already dealers. "We looked at those that wanted changing and those that could be developed," says Putnam. "Over the following three years, we gradually fine tuned that." The attitude was tough, but Putnam is certain that it was right. "I don't care how good your product is. I don't care how good your intentions are, as a manufacturer, if you do not have a strong, dedicated and professional dealer network, then everything you do is short-term.

You have no control on your business because the prime interface between your customer and your company is through your dealer network if you're in the car business. If that ain't right, then you're wasting your time."

While the new moves came as a shock to the dealers, they were not much more welcome at Austin-Rover. Every Jaguar dealer was also an Austin-Rover dealer and, in some cases, it was the Jaguar franchise that was keeping the dealerships afloat. Some dealers depended on Jaguar for as much as 40 per cent of their revenue. When that franchise was removed, businesses failed. Some senior Austin-Rover managers conceded that the programme was right for Jaguar but criticised the fact that dealers were left to go bankrupt. Sadly, that is more a reflection on the viability of the Austin-Rover franchise than a condemnation of Jaguar's actions.

At that time, there was a joint franchise operations committee, and Putnam would tell the Austin-Rover managers what he was doing. He admits that ". . . it got very steamy from time to time". Putnam believes that the Austin-Rover people could not understand what he was doing or what he was trying to achieve. It might be that his strategy of achieving increased sales by reducing the number of dealers was so alien to them that they could not comprehend it. Some of their antagonism was certainly due to the fact that old friends were being forced out of business. But Putnam had no allegiances within the network and had only one goal in view: to build a good dealer network for Jaguar.

Some dealers did not believe the message about a new approach to the franchise. Neil Johnson explains: "They were sitting back, smiling benignly, saying, 'We've seen all this before. All we've got to do is pick up the 'phone to Trevor or Tony or Ray or whoever and we'll get all this stopped, because it's all too silly for words.' I felt that we had to do something to focus their attention on the reality of the problem and, at the end of the day, it has to be money. You can talk until you're blue in the face, but unless there's a financial dimension, it doesn't actually hit them between the eyes." Out of that realisation was born the franchise development fund, which was paid for by cutting the discounts provided to dealers. Roger Putnam appears to have reached the same conclusion by another route. His concern centred on price cutting by the dealers.

When a Jaguar was sold, the dealer would be given a discount of 17.5 per cent off list price. That was his profit margin. However, in order to sell cars, dealers were offering discounts of up to 12.5 per cent to the customer, leaving 5 per cent retained gross profit. That had two effects. It debased the product in the market place, and it reduced the second-hand values of Jaguars, which were bad enough already because of poor quality. Discounting new cars meant that when buyers came to sell them, they got much less money for them than they expected. This was a problem Putnam had already experienced at Lotus; he had overcome it by cutting the discounts. By doing so he forced them to think carefully before offering discounts to their customers. The paradoxical result was that retained margins increased. In July, Putnam outlined to Johnson his plan to reduce discounting by cutting dealer margins.

He suggested alternative uses for the money, because it was clear that the network would never agree to Jaguar simply hanging on to it. One of these was to implement a programme of minimum standards that each dealership would be expected to achieve in exterior signage, showroom decor, presentation, sales training, service facilities, advertising and so on. There was nothing new about the concept. BLEO had tried to implement a similar programme in 1980, but Putnam says that when he arrived at Jaguar in 1982, no Jaguar dealers had implemented any part of it. He thought cash would help to encourage them to improve standards.

So a franchise development fund was created by holding back 3.5 per cent of the dealers' discounts. Dealers who achieved the minimum standards received cash payments. Neil Johnson announced this decision at a Jaguar dealer council meeting late in 1982. He had explained it to the chairman beforehand, but no one else knew about it outside the factory. "I gave them my word that none of that money would be clawed back into Jaguar. It would all be pumped back into the network, but only into the network that worked for it. There was stunned silence when I announced it." Nevertheless, it was accepted.

The scheme was introduced during the first quarter of 1983, and it was not long before dealers began to see the results. "As dealers improved their showroom, service reception, training and all the rest of it, every time they did something they were supposed to do, they got a tick and they actually got money too," Johnson explains. But some dealers received nothing. In the main these were the large groups. Some worked on the principle that they would try the new standards in one showroom and leave the rest alone. As a result, in a town where there were two dealers but only enough business for one, it was often the independent who saw the opportunities and qualified for payments. Johnson recalls: "My 'phone nearly melted with chairmen of these groups saying, 'Yes, we voted for it, but we didn't think it was going to affect us,' or 'Yes, dear boy, of course I supported you. Absolutely laudable aim, but you can't seriously include us in it.'"

Egan recalls seeing representatives from a big group that owned about 16 Jaguar dealerships. They told him that the minimum standards were too expensive. They were prepared to try them in one or two outlets, but he could forget any ideas he had of seeing them in the rest. They said they had been selling Jaguars for BL for many years and would continue to do what they had always done.

Egan then said, "Well, that's fine then. That's the end of that."

"What do you mean?" asked the group's managing director.

"I'd like all the franchises back," said Egan.

There was a pause. "What," said the managing director, "all 16?"

"Every one," replied Egan. "As far as I'm concerned, they've all gone. We've got plenty of people who are willing to put money into the franchise. That's what it's going to be. We'll take the lot."

The managing director and his colleagues sat in stunned horror for a few minutes and then said, "We'll do the minimum standards."

"No, no," replied Egan. "I'm not even sure that's what we want now. I think you're better off leaving them all."

In fact, the group retained about six dealerships, and that was reduced to four later. Another large group that came under scrutiny was Henly's, which is generally credited with having helped William Lyons to build the Jaguar business in the first place by placing large orders with him. During this franchising review, Henly's itself was acquired by the Hawley Group. Under the terms of the dealership agreement, Jaguar had the right to withdraw the franchise in the case of a change of ownership. It did exactly that. Every Henly's Jaguar dealer was fired. At one time, Henly's had had 37 Jaguar outlets, although that had been greatly reduced by its own programme of closures. Ultimately, three franchises were reprieved. The bloodletting brought a Henly's representative to see Putnam who was based, at that time, in temporary offices at Whitley, near Coventry. "The guy couldn't believe what I'd done," Putnam says. The Henly's man remarked on Putnam's temporary accommodation. "I said that I was very happy because my previous office had been in the old safe . . . walls about 10 feet thick, and it was very hot in there. He said, 'Doing your job, I can understand why you lived in a safe.' He was not amused."

In general, however, Putnam maintains that the programme was carried through with a remarkable lack of acrimony. "Even though we were at daggers drawn, it was all done with enormous decorum." Putnam gives the impression that he did not care what anyone thought. His one objective, which he was determined to reach, was a completely restructured dealer network. By the time the XJ40 was launched in the autumn of 1986, 50 of the original 300 dealers remained. Egan is in no doubt about who drove the programme through. "I think he pushed it along with more force and leadership than I would have done. I wasn't sure that it was possible. He was more sure than I was and he got on with it himself."

Putnam admits that he was lucky in some respects. "One of the greatest aids that I had was that I didn't need to grow the market in volume terms. North America was taking as many cars as we could ship. I didn't, therefore, need to grow the UK, but as we cut down the number of dealers, the volume grew automatically." This is an oversimplification; cutting the number of dealers was only one part of a complex programme. Even so, in Putnam's words, "5,000 (cars) through 300 dealers changed to 8,000 through 110 dealers, so there was a vast change in their fortunes."

A key aspect of the plan was that every level of management was committed to it. No one could circumvent it by appealing to someone further up the tree. This was an important feature of the new management team. When it made a decision, it stood by it, at all levels. As the new dealer network was created, attention turned to the way in which it was operated. One aspect of the business was driven home to Putnam when he called to see the Derbyshire BMW dealer, Frank Sytner. "There, sitting on his showroom floor, was one of my bigger midlands dealer's demonstrators, that I'd seen parked outside his showroom not two weeks before. 'What the hell's that doing here?' I asked, and he said, 'He sold it to us.'"

Putnam realised that for various reasons – lack of entrepreneurial thrust, snobbery, laziness – the dealers were not selling used cars at retail. They were selling them to other dealers who would then sell them to the public. Not only were they missing a profit opportunity; Jaguar had no control over prices for used cars. Putnam introduced a used car programme to encourage dealers to sell used cars themselves and worked on the trader's price guide, *Glass's Guide*, with the aim of persuading the publisher to improve the prices recommended for used Jaguars and Daimlers. In time, used cars became an integral part of the franchise with a special section in the *Sunday Times* and mechanical breakdown insurance.

But the used car programme was still in the future when Putnam turned his attention to the professionalism of the salesmen themselves. Johnson asked him to put together a salesman's club and Putnam, who wanted to begin serious sales training, responded with alacrity. But he did not want the salesmen to move on to sell BMWs or Porsches once they had been trained. So Peter Battam, through the communications agency KLP, put together the Jaguar Foundation. This is a salesman's club in everything but name, and involves incentive programmes and grants. The first stage was to enrol the salesmen; every dealer was told that there had to be at least one specialist Jaguar salesman. Putnam says the inital reaction was hostile. "We'll have rebellion, mutiny among our salesmen. They all like selling Jaguars," he was told. Putnam's response was characteristically blunt. "But they're not selling them. They all like to give away Jaguars." Slowly he persuaded the dealers to register their salesmen. Then he committed what many dealer principals regarded as the sin of communicating direct with the salesmen. There was uproar from some dealers, but Putnam ignored it and carried on. "When the first two bulletins had arrived and they'd realised we were not inciting the guys to riot, the thing just went away." He adds: "They began to see that we were going to do it whether they liked it or not, that was also clear."

The stability of the team was crucial in these developments. Dealers had become accustomed to the BLEO way of working and, before that, to Leyland Cars methods. BL companies had been in almost constant upheaval. Reorganisation had become a way of life. As one former manager puts it: "If we didn't have a reorganisation for six months, we'd begin to wonder what was going on. Everything was constantly changing. If your own job didn't change, your boss probably would." In Jaguar's sales and marketing organisation, Johnson was looking for stability. "I think it was nearly three years before anybody changed," he says. "It was regularly commented on by the network – how nice to see the same person two conferences in a row. It was very important."

But Johnson did change the product line in 1983, when the Jaguar Sovereign was announced. The change was prompted when he arrived at the factory one morning and realised that all the other directors drove Daimlers, which had more luxurious trim and better interior fitments. He was the only director who drove a Jaguar and that was because he used an XJ-S. He admits that, had there been a Daimler version of that, he would probably have been driving a Daimler too. At the time, however, the company was in the curious position of being called Jaguar but selling more Daimlers than anything else. The reason was obvious. "Everything you could possibly have done to produce an Austin in a Jaguar body had been done with the Jaguar."

At the next board meeting, Johnson advocated a special edition Jaguar. That was greeted with dismay because special edition cars are traditionally used to try and stimulate the sales of ageing product lines. Johnson compounded his sin by saying that he wanted to call the car the Jaguar Sovereign. The purists pointed out that Sovereign was a Daimler name, but Johnson was undeterred. He had instructed the experimental shop to produce a Jaguar with a Daimler interior, but Jaguar seats. "I parked it in the old showroom at Browns Lane, and when everybody was getting worked up, I just said, 'Right, come and have a look at the car.' Howls of disbelief, but John bought it straightaway."

The original intention was to build only 1,000, but Egan suggested that it should go through as a full-blown product change. The new car was announced at the same time as Jaguar dropped the Vanden Plas name in the UK. The range was now the Jaguar XJ6 and XJ12, the Jaguar Sovereign with either a six- or a 12-cylinder engine, and the Daimler with the same engine choice. "It all fitted rather nicely," Johnson says. "We had the XJ6 for the bottom of the line; we had the Jaguar Sovereign for the senior manager, board member, main board executive or whatever, and we had the Daimler for the chairman. So instead of having two bites of the cherry, we had three, potentially."

The Sovereign, he maintains, was taking 75 per cent of XJ saloon sales within a short time with ". . . tremendous profit implications." He believes there have been discussions about discontinuing Daimler, but is convinced that the company needs the Daimler marque. In his view, Daimler should be moved closer to Bentley. The Vanden Plas name, on the other hand, was dropped in the UK, because of the way BL had used it. "Vanden Plas was a badge that was appearing on everything that Austin-Rover was making," David Boole says, "so the Vanden Plas image for something at the top end of the Jaguar line-up was inappropriate."

By this time, Egan was being promoted in the media as the head of Jaguar, to give the company an identifiable face and a clear leadership. Boole comments: "The company, for so many years, had been built up around the personality of Sir William

Lyons, prior to the British Leyland years and I thought, for that reason, it was sensible that there should be an identifiable figurehead for the company." There was another consideration: Boole suspected that the company was to be privatised, and he felt that it would benefit from having a widely recognised chief executive. His train of thought, however, seems to have been in marked contrast to that of the BL board.

The privatisation was announced in 1984, and it was decided that a new chairman was needed for Jaguar Cars Holdings, which was to be floated as Jaguar plc. Horrocks had been chairman but he was needed to run Austin-Rover. The man who was appointed was Hamish Orr-Ewing. The privatisation was a great success (see Chapter 9), but Orr-Ewing subsequently became convinced that Jaguar faced grave dangers. These fell into two main areas. First, Jaguar was dependent for an increasing proportion of its sales on the American market and it was, basically, a one product company. Although it made the XJ-S and the Daimler limousine, the great majority of its sales were of XJ saloons. Any manufacturer in such a position is walking a tightrope. If the American market went into decline, the company would suffer. Similarly, another fuel crisis could have catastrophic effects.

The second consideration was this: when the company was floated, it was protected from takeover by the fact that the government held a "golden share", but this protection was due to run out in 1990. Ford, General Motors and BMW had all made approaches to Jaguar, and had been rebuffed, but once the golden share disappeared, Jaguar would be vulnerable. Companies such as General Motors were searching for a prestige car maker to buy, and were in a position to pay almost any price.

The conviction grew in Orr-Ewing's mind that Jaguar should explore one of two possibilities. Either it could acquire other businesses to give itself a broader base, or it could look for a collaborator within the motor industry. Immediately after being floated, Jaguar had appointed Morgan Grenfell as its new merchant bank and Orr-Ewing went to see its chairman along wih the two non-executive directors: Horrocks and Ted Bond. According to Horrocks, they discussed these concerns but came to no conclusion. None of the executive directors agreed that the company's business base should be widened. Egan maintains that many successful car companies have diversified and run into trouble. Indeed, this had happened at Jaguar in the 1960s. Orr-Ewing appears to have underestimated the strength of feeling about the proposals that he was discussing, although Egan empha-sises that he tried to persuade Orr-Ewing to abandon them on at least two occasions. Orr-Ewing then began to talk to Morgan Grenfell about the desirability of appointing additional non-executive directors. That would have tilted the balance of the board in favour of the non-executive directors.

Some time later, Horrocks told the Jaguar board that he would be unable to attend its next meeting because he had to go to Japan on Austin-Rover business. He heard the result of the meeting in the departure lounge of Narita airport, in Tokyo: Egan had ousted Orr-Ewing as chairman. Horrocks was amazed because there had been no suggestion that Orr-Ewing was about to resign. He heard Orr-Ewing's version of events while he was in America, on his way back to Britain. According to Horrocks, Orr-Ewing told him that, as soon as the meeting had begun, Egan had proposed a vote of no confidence in the chairman on the basis that he had been "acting not in the best interests of Jaguar". Orr-Ewing was shocked but took a vote on the motion. The board was split equally between executive and non-executive directors. The executive directors were Egan himself, Graham Whitehead, who ran Jaguar Inc. in the US and finance director John Edwards. The non-executive directors were Orr-Ewing, Bond and Horrocks. Horrocks had written to Orr-Ewing, explaining his absence and asking the chairman to speak for him.

Egan's move was a dangerous gamble. If he had lost the vote, his position would have been untenable. The fact that he proposed the motion suggests that he was sure of the support of the executive directors, but he could still have been defeated if the others had voted against, because Orr-Ewing had a casting vote. In the event, Bond did nothing. Orr-Ewing produced Horrocks's letter, but this was ruled to be not a valid form of proxy by a lawyer who was in an adjacent room. So the motion was carried. Orr-Ewing had no choice but to step down, and Egan was voted in as chairman.

The news broke on March 2, 1985, and was reported in the press the following day. Although the event was presented as a decision by Orr-Ewing, who had supposedly decided that Jaguar's ". . . executive management is fully capable of controlling its destiny", some suspected other reasons for the change. Kenneth Gooding in the *Financial Times* appears to have been particularly suspicious. His report referred to ". . . problems which have obviously arisen between Mr Orr-Ewing and Mr Egan . . ." Both Orr-Ewing and Horrocks resigned from the board in April.

When Egan was installed as chairman, the XJ40 was still 18 months from launch, and much had still to be done in terms of franchise development in Europe and investment in the company. In Europe, the most important market was West Germany, the biggest market for luxury cars outside America. Jaguar sales in Germany in 1982 stood at just 845. As product improvements came through, sales climbed, to nearly 2,000 in 1984 and 2,350 in 1985. Neil Johnson claims that the German market had been neglected for years. In deciding what to do about that, he considered three options. "One was a complete takeover, where we would run our own company with our own staff," he says. "One was that we should simply appoint an outstanding distributor who would do the job, full stop and we would just export to that market. The third was a compromise between the two – which was the one we eventually went for." The partner that was chosen was the company's Swiss importer, Emil Frey. Jaguar Deutschland was formed as a joint venture. Jaguar held 35 per cent of the equity, Frey held the rest. The company was installed in a new complex at Frankfurt in 1985, and began trying to achieve in Germany, the franchising results that had been brought about in Britain.

Since 1980, Jaguar has achieved much, and the launch of the XJ40 in 1986 (see Chapter 10) was obviously a landmark. But there is no sense of complacency at Browns Lane. As product engineering director Jim Randle said recently, "The thing about success is that its very hard. If you're successful, people expect

you to be more successful and the only way you can do that
is by working harder and harder, making better and better
products, because nothing is ever good enough. Success is a
hard taskmaster.''

CHAPTER 5
Build Them Better

The number of people who claim to have begun to attack Jaguar's quality problems is legion. That quality was deficient for a long time is no secret. Jaguars were for years known as superbly designed cars that should have been better developed and built. Yet, until recently, the pattern was to launch new models long before they were ready and try to catch up on the development programme later. Until the late 1960s, the company managed to get away with that, but the XJ6 moved it into a new market, a market that expected better things from its cars and so the poor quality began to have an effect.

Even so, this did not have much impact on the company until the mid-1970s, by which time quality was actually declining. The cause of the decline was relatively complex. At Jaguar, the point is made frequently that the design of the cars was good. Apart from one or two aberrations, this is undoubtedly true, but there is no doubt, either, that early customers for each new model would find themselves in the position of completing the testing of the car. This was not unique to Jaguar. For years, the British motor industry consistently launched cars before they were fully developed. Until the late 1970s, car buyers would often refuse to consider a new model until it had been on sale for at least a year, until the manufacturer had "got the bugs sorted out".

What did set Jaguar apart, however, is that the engineering department, under the leadership of Bob Knight, was more interested in designing the next car than it was in eliminating defects in current ones. One former colleague says: "I don't think Bob had all that much interest in the current car. He much preferred to figure out what was going on with the next car, almost to the point of burying his head in the sand." The result was that the next new model would often take priority over quality problems that required engineering solutions. Customers would find faults, but the company was less diligent than it should have been in rectifying them.

Unfortunately, new cars were not always designed to be easy to build. This question has probably caused more friction between engineering departments and manufacturing departments in car companies than anything else. In the mid-1970s David Simpson, who was plant director at Browns Lane for a time, recalls: "We had to try to get an understanding that an engineering solution was not always suitable to manufacturing." Mike Beasley is another who remembers that manufacturing and engineering tended to follow different tracks. "Manufacturing people beavered away at solving manufacturing, or perceived manufacturing problems. Engineering, in their own way, tried to resolve the engineering problems, things that were fed to them by BL as engineering problems. But there was never any pulling together, or a common effort to say, 'Look, we have a problem here, we must resolve it', and sitting down as a team and finding the best way to resolve it."

This points to the heart of the quality issue. Quality has to be designed into a car from the beginning. If it is not, no amount of inspection and haranguing of suppliers and workforce can build it in. Quality is not a surface gloss. It is fundamental to a car. This was not widely understood before the late 1970s. Car manufacturers would work on the basis that quality could be improved by a combination of inspectors and rectification bays. There was a general failure to see that if the design job was done right in the first place, the rectification bays should not have been needed.

But these were not the only causes of Jaguar's reputation for poor quality and unreliability. Geoffrey Robinson's drive for increased volume also led to a fall in standards. Although the rate at which cars are built can be increased, it has to be done carefully if there is not to be a fall in build quality. If the rate of production is stepped up, people will tend to cut corners, or they might not have the time to do their jobs with as much care as they should. There was also the effect of falling morale. Jaguar employees were proud of the product and the company. With the erosion of

Jaguar's independence during the early 1970s, the workforce became steadily more demoralised. When Leyland Cars was formed, morale at the factory fell even further, particularly when employees learnt that the factory was not even to carry the name Jaguar any more. By the time Egan arrived in 1980, spirits could fall no lower. The assembly workers were on strike, although they had been threatened with dismissal. Egan: "The Jaguar workers were saying, 'Well, you've done everything else to us, so you might as well close us down.'"

When employees have been pushed that far, the chances of them achieving high assembly standards are remote. But the aspects discussed so far are only 40 per cent of the explanation. Components suppliers also bore a substantial responsibility. Today, Jaguar people maintain that their purchasing power was constrained by their relatively low volumes. "We had to take what was available," one says. "If we needed a 75-amp alternator and the biggest available was 60 amps, then that was all we could get." Components suppliers were operating in the same way as the car manufacturers themselves. They were making products and then expecting their sales force to sell them. There was little, if any, attempt, to find out what the market wanted and then supply it. Doubtless the 60-amp alternator was big enough for the manufacturing giants, and so the supplier saw no reason to vary the specification for a minnow like Jaguar.

Even granting that that was so, however, one has to question the wisdom of designing an electrical system that requires a component that is not available. Furthermore, Jaguar, in common with other car manufacturers, operated a purchasing policy that has been dubbed the "black box" approach. A manufacturer would go to a component supplier and request, say, a distributor that had to be within certain dimensions and to meet certain technical specifications. Provided the distributor met the criteria, the company would accept it and was unlikely to think any further about its quality.

Some components gained appalling reputations. The Series II XJ6, for example, used a type of switch on the fascia known as push/push because they were pushed to switch equipment on and again to switch it off. Time and again, these proved defective. Geoffrey Robinson went to see Lucas, the manufacturer to complain. "The things fell out. They came apart," he says. "I'm not an engineer, but you could see the crass quality of it. It was very evident that we weren't anywhere near exigent enough."

The quality question was a complex one. The idea that poor quality was entirely attributable to suppliers, is plainly untrue. They carried some of the blame, but by no means all of it.

One man who made a serious attempt to improve quality was recruited early in 1975. Charles Maple had been quality assurance director of fighting vehicles with the Ministry of Defence. Stokes appointed him director of quality for the Leyland group in May 1975. Maple was responsible for many quality initiatives in Leyland Cars as a whole, and at Jaguar in particular. One of the first big efforts was Quality '77, which was aimed at persuading employees to think about quality as something that mattered. Whether it achieved anything is debatable. A tendency to believe that poor quality was someone else's fault was a general failing at that time. Manufacturing blamed engineering. Engineering blamed manufacturing. The assembly workers blamed the managers. The managers blamed the workforce and the suppliers. No one would admit to any share of the blame.

Maple tried to attack that tendency by taking cars at random from the production line at Browns Lane. His inspectors would check them and highlight faults. They were shown to senior managers, who would be harangued by Maple. Defective cars were also displayed around the factory for the workforce to see, yet it seems to have had little effect. What Maple could not change was employees' low morale. If the workforce did not care, there would be no change.

Beasley says that despite Maple's programme, quality remained a low priority for BL managers at plant level, in comparison with cost performance. "People's minds were not focused on the fact that you were making rubbish cars. Other objectives were of a higher order. Leyland Cars did not focus on the fact that quality was vital, not at a plant level, anyway. Whether that aspiration was up there with Whittaker and the others, I don't know, but certainly, by the time it got to the plant, that was not a clear objective. Charles Maple banged his head against a lot of brick walls."

After Michael Edwardes took over as BL chairman in 1977, Maple was asked to devise a system of technical audits. David Andrews, the group's executive vice-chairman from 1978 to 1982 says: "The idea of a technical audit was to test the adequacy of the technical processes, both of the finished product and of the key steps that led towards it – be it a design, development or manufacturing process, engineering or actual handling practices." The audit staff reported to the main board, and the system produced frictions, partly because it showed up operational short-comings, and partly because it was novel. "People were used to financial auditors coming in," Andrews observes, "but technical audits really offended against the manhood. They showed that you hadn't been doing your drawings properly or you hadn't been executing the product properly. The evidence was there to see."

The technical audits went to senior managers and provided detailed information on aspects of the company that were not working properly. "It meant getting down to what the foreman was doing and what the individual operators were doing," Andrews explains. "Changing the overalls they wore so that they didn't have buttons on and scratch things, how they slung bodies, a myriad of detailed items." While Maple's auditors were identifying bad practices that caused poor quality, Jaguar-Rover-Triumph managers were trying to overcome their most pressing difficulties. Of these, the paint plant was clearly the worst, because a car's paint is so visible. A company can get away with repetitive faults on a component for a while, but not with a poor body finish. Pratt Thompson, head of JRT and later of BL International, recalls: "It was all acrimony. There was so much of the mentality of blaming the other guy instead of sitting down and solving the problems. This was part of the inheritance. It had gone on for years." He tried to avoid simply pointing the finger at suppliers. Discussions with Lucas took place "at a fairly high level, and with a fair amount of goodwill". The approach adopted was: "What is the problem? How did it arise? How quickly are we going to be able to fix it? We'll sort out who pays for it later. We want to stay in business in the meantime."

Maple also began to implement management policy instruction number seven (MPI7), which was an important departure from established practice. It placed an onus on the supplier to approve the design and use of a component. If the manufacturer was demanding a design or an installation that would jeopardise the reliability of a component, the supplier had the responsibility to refuse to supply. But the implementation of MPI7 was to be a long process. As Jaguar engineering director Jim Randle explains: "MPI7 works if you have someone as competent or more competent than yourself at the other end." Randle believes that in the early years, suppliers were probably not able to judge whether a specification or an installation was likely to cause a quality or reliability problem. Some suppliers undoubtedly permitted their components to be used in unsuitable ways.

Despite these initiatives, Jaguar quality standards were still judged to be poor by customers when Egan arrived in 1980. A report from J. D. Power, the US market research company, indicated that barely a fifth of Jaguar's American customers were satisfied with their cars 35 days after taking delivery of them.

The current management, and Egan in particular, has been credited with turning the company around by improving quality standards. That is an oversimplification, but there is no doubt that Egan and his team showed a determination to improve quality greater than that of any other BL management to that time. And, as Beasley points out, "if quality is your driving force, the cost performances and all the other good things that one uses in industry tend to come anyway". One of the ways in which manufacturers try to measure their performance in terms of construction quality is by using a quality index (QI). This involves taking a car from the track and examining it carefully for faults. Each fault found attracts a penalty, the size of which depends on its gravity. Beasley recalls that the attitude to QIs changed after Egan arrived. "We set about measuring them more objectively," he says. "We were getting scores which were very low and which we weren't very proud of. We measured Mercedes-Benz and BMW cars, set some milestones and some yardsticks and we showed all of the workforce and the management." This was part of the process of explaining to everybody that Jaguar had to improve. "There was an attitude around that suggested Jaguar lived on its myth, not on its reality," Beasley explains. "One thing John did very effectively was to bring that to a violently sudden halt and face people with reality."

Perhaps the biggest test of the company's commitment to improving quality was the choice that had to be made between developing the new XJ40 and eradicating faults on existing series III saloons. The company did not have the resources to do both simultaneously. When Egan arrived, XJ40 was due for launch in 1983, but achieving that deadline would have meant that everybody had to work flat out on that alone. As Egan presented the question, Beasley says the choice was simple. "He faced everybody with the fact that we were going to go out of business unless we fixed some problems." Series III won. "We sat down and looked at the size of the problem first," Jim Randle says. "We examined where the problems were. Once we'd established that the car we'd got was reasonable if we built it right, it was a matter of deciding what we should do to try and get it right and that included things like taking over the Castle Bromwich plant."

Egan began discussions with dealers whom he felt he could trust. One of these was Alan Clark of Colliers, a Birmingham dealer that had taken on the Jaguar franchise in 1972. Egan explained his belief that the company and the cars were worth saving and admitted that something had to be done about quality. "John said that he was going to get people to concentrate on bits of the car," Clark recalls. "He had problems inside the company and outside with suppliers. Part of the trouble came from poor dealers, of course." Task forces were set up to identify where things had gone wrong, and 10 individuals were seconded from their normal jobs to co-ordinate the effort. One of these was Jonathan Heynes. He was made responsible for organising approaches to suppliers under the supervision of quality director David Fielden. According to Heynes, around 750 problems were identified as needing urgent and authoritative attention.

In the early days, the co-ordinating team had no offices, but then space near the boardroom became available. Egan suggested that the boardroom should be used for meetings with suppliers. That was to prove psychologically important. "If you ask a supplier to come to a meeting in the boardroom at 8.30 in the morning, he tends to come," Heynes says. The boardroom was also close to Egan's office and he would pass the door on his way to other parts of the factory. He took to dropping in, to ask how things were going and to add his authority to the efforts of the team. Heynes maintains that 40 per cent of troubles identified were cured in under six months, in most cases without great difficulty. The next 40 per cent required design changes and took much longer. The remainder were judged impossible to eliminate. Some of the most intractable difficulties involved electrical systems, and here, Lucas had to be involved. Geoff Clayden, Lucas quality manager, brought senior managers from five Lucas companies to meetings in the boardroom at Browns Lane every Friday morning for eight months.

By the end of the first year, progress had been good enough for the original task force to be reduced to five people. Confidence in the company's ability to improve quality had risen so far that the press launch of the HE engine included an admission that cars built in 1979 and 1980 had been of poor quality. David Boole claims that this caused concern within BL. "Everybody else in the corporation was saying you should never admit that you've built bad cars," he says. In fact, the corporation had been admitting to its dealers that it had done so since the mid-1970s – but promised that quality was now improving. However, a different face may have been put on things for the benefit of the press.

Boole was well aware of the risks involved. "I told John Egan: 'I know you've made lots of progress, but this is the sort of thing that you can do only once. If you are going to communicate the improved quality to the outside world, there are several things of importance. One is that it must be based on fact. Clearly, to a large extent, it is. Lots of improvements have been made. But secondly, it's not the sort of thing that you can keep doing.

You're on a treadmill from there on. You have to keep delivering improved quality. Hopefully, the quality will continually improve. People will give you one opportunity to try and promulgate this message, but after that, you have to live up to it.' Fortunately, we were able to do that.''

Referring to bad quality in the past was in some ways an odd tactic because, according to Boole, the press was not as aware of the prevalence of faults as dealers and owners. Generally speaking, if a journalist drove a Jaguar, it was provided by the factory and was meticulously prepared. Journalists did not have the same long-term involvement with cars as owners. Obviously, they heard from their readers and from friends about poor Jaguar quality, but Boole reckons that they were, at worst, sceptical about the products. Yet, the best way to communicate the improvements to customers was through the press. If the message was to have any credence with the growing band of disaffected owners, trying to say that Jaguars were even better was a waste of time. Owners would not believe that any improvement had been made if the company tried to imply that there had been nothing wrong with the cars in the first place.

Owners' opinions began to be channelled directly into Jaguar from the end of 1982, when Joe Greenwell joined the sales and marketing department. Ever since the late 1970s a consumer satisfaction index (CSI) had been compiled by the BL marketing research department. Greenwell transferred the Jaguar section of it to Browns Lane towards the end of 1982. The CSI is operated in the UK, West Germany, the US, Canada and Australia. Independent research companies, of which J. D. Power is one, are commissioned to send out letters to customers explaining that they might be contacted by telephone, and asking for their co-operation as part of the company's research into customer satisfaction. Every month, the research company calls up to 150 customers in the UK 33 days after they have taken delivery of their cars to conduct an interview. The numbers contacted in the other markets vary, but Greenwell maintains that it is always enough to provide a statistically valid sample.

The interview lasts around 45 minutes and establishes the

customer's detailed ratings of various aspects of the car. The researcher also covers fault analysis on key warranty areas and demographic details of the customer. There is a follow-up after nine months and again after 18 months. Graham Whitehead, who has run the company's American operation for many years, has no doubts about the value of this research. Shortly after the CSI programme was transferred to Jaguar, the company decided to impose a more stringent regime on its suppliers. Faulty components were costing Jaguar a lot of money. Some costs were, of course, recovered. When a part was replaced under warranty, the dealer who replaced it would return it to Jaguar, which would pass it back to the supplier. The supplier would be charged the cost of the part. But neither the cost of the labour involved in changing it, nor the cost of returning it, was recovered. The new approach involved telling suppliers that, as long as warranty claims on their components were less than 1.5 per cent, they would still be charged only the original equipment price. Once the warranty rate climbed above 1.5 per cent, however, Jaguar would want labour costs on all parts changed. Since labour in the US cost around $40 an hour, and five hours were allowed to change a starter motor, that was a powerful incentive to suppliers to improve reliability. As Heynes puts it: "It focused the minds of our suppliers on the fact that warranty is their responsibility."

But Jaguar did not merely try to beat suppliers into providing what it wanted. The company actively helped them to improve. In 1985, Egan was quoted as saying that its engineers spent as much as 20 per cent of their time helping suppliers to redesign products. It was in 1985, too, that the company began to hand out accolades as well as brickbats. The "Supplier of the Year" award has been announced every December since then and the company that is chosen receives a trophy and features in a full page press advertisement. Others that have achieved high standards receive "Pursuit of Excellence" awards. By this time, the results were coming through in CSI findings. In 1984, J. D. Power reported that 90 per cent of American owners were satisfied with their cars 35 days after taking delivery. Only Mercedes-Benz achieved a better result. In 1985, Jaguar again came second in the table. A year later, it dropped to sixth in terms of customer satisfaction. Even so, it was still ahead of BMW and Porsche.

But while much was being achieved with suppliers and within the factory, one of the most important developments was the rebirth of the pride that the workforce had once had in Jaguar. To achieve this, a "hearts and minds" programme was launched not long after Egan's arrival; it began with a series of Jaguar nights out – social events aimed at creating a friendlier atmosphere and at showing what Jaguar as a whole was about. Employees from each plant, and their families, could learn more about what the people at the other two did. These social evenings took place at the factories and ran for around nine months. They were so successful that the company began to hold open days, "fun runs" and bonfire parties as well. Mike Kinsky has been heavily involved in the programme since its inception. He explains that hearts and minds was part of a wider range of activities aimed at recruiting, integrating, training and developing employees, structuring the organisation for them to work in and, finally, providing pre-retirement training. Kinsky credits Egan with initiating the programme: "He got the workforce together, committed to a common aim, which was about survival and satisfying customers."

This was done by ensuring that the workforce was kept informed about progress made in turning the company round. Magazines, briefing documents and video programmes were all used to provide information. Quality circles were formed, in Kinsky's words, ". . . to make sure people could feed information back up as well as cascading it down". Jaguar's approach to training seems to have changed markedly, too. Traditionally, car manufacturers have provided training that is more or less job-specific. People on the factory floor are trained in the use of new machinery. Managers might be trained in management skills or given the opportunity to learn a second language, if they need it. Kinsky describes this approach as "reactive". A need is defined, then training is provided to meet it. At Jaguar, however, every employee has the opportunity to take various courses, all of which are, to some degree, job-related. Any employee can enrol for any course, provided he or she can meet the entry criteria for those courses that require some prior qualification.

The range of courses is similar to that offered by any responsible company. What makes Jaguar's "open learning programme" unusual is that the courses are mostly run in the evenings and so employees have to make a commitment in terms of their own time. Kinsky points out counselling is provided to help employees choose appropriate courses, but in principle the decision is theirs. "If you wanted to enter for a City and Guilds craft course in numerical control, and you were a finance man, we'd say, 'Well, don't you think it's better that you consider something else?' So there is a selection process, but it's not to put people off, it's to try to channel them into the appropriate thing for their own development."

He points out that there is considerable scope for individuals to set their own goals, citing two middle-aged men from the factory who were on a GCE O-level mathematics course visited by Egan. The company chief asked them why they were doing it. One wanted to keep up with his grandson's school work. The other said that he had to learn maths to programme his new machine, but he wanted to become a manufacturing engineer. He had to gain his O-level, then A-level, then study for a part-time degree with Jaguar. "I know I'll be 50 but that's what I want to do." Kinsky is adamant that the man would be given all the assistance he needed to follow the courses through. He claims that the open learning programme has been so successful that, by 1986, the average employee was receiving about five days of off-job training every year. The cost to Jaguar represented 2 per cent of turnover at a time when the average in industry was 0.5 per cent.

The company clearly believes that employee training is a critical part of its development programme. That applies at management levels too. However, the company's management of its managers has had to develop over the years. Many managers who were involved in the early period after Egan arrived speak of the excitement of these years. Events were moving quickly and there was an entrepreneurial spirit in the company. Today, Jaguar has grown. The flotation has meant that attitudes have had to change. From a management point of view, one of the most important factors is that the company is not growing at its former rate. (Turnover grew from £192.5 million in 1981 to £305.6 million in 1982. From 1985 to 1986, the increase was from £746.5 million to £830.4 million.) This means that, if people are not to grow stale, because of diminished promotion prospects, or be tempted to leave for the same reason, some other way must be found to motivate them. Kinsky believes the answer is job rotation.

"There's a fundamental belief in the company that people can do more than one job," Kinsky says, "and it's all down to good management skills. Good managers can actually lead most departments." He admits that in some cases, department heads must have technical knowledge, but is adamant that management skills are more important. "You always have your technical specialists in functions, whether chartered accountants or design engineers," he says. "But when you actually get to departments, you want people who can lead people. You want good line managers. You want people who can make things happen, can control things and utilise the expertise of those who work for them."

For that approach to work, it is obviously necessary for Jaguar to provide a high degree of management training. Some courses, such as the part-time master of business administration course, are organised with the help of Warwick University in Coventry. But the basis of management training are courses that Kinsky describes as "almost mandatory". These supervisory and management effectiveness programmes take three weeks: one week of course work, a week back at work with a project to complete, and a final week of course work. Jaguar ran courses at its own factories for a few years before concerns arose about their introverted nature. At that point the company turned to the Cranfield Institute of Technology, largely because of the institute's involvement in the motor industry. Middle management is put through a two-week course there. Judging by the experience of Joe Greenwell, who has been on the course, the benefit is not only enhanced knowledge, but also the relationships that are built with other managers. "What it did was to forge great bonds across functions," Greenwell says. "It wrought tremendous bonds with people who were on the course with you. What they then did was to harness that and use it. They built multi-discipline project teams and threw them at problems."

Today, Jaguar seems to spend almost as much time breaking down barriers between departments as it once did on cracking quality problems on the XJ6. There is general recognition of the fact that the departments will achieve more if they devote their energies to fighting the competition instead of one another. One insider comments: "We work as a team, even if we are at each other's throats sometimes." That has played a part in improving quality too. There is less temptation to blame someone else and more incentive to take the initiative in overcoming difficulties.

CHAPTER 6
Success in the States

The US is Jaguar's most important single export market, and is certain to remain so because of its sheer size. Some observers maintain that about three quarters of the people in the world who can afford to buy a Jaguar live in America. Even so, the company tried until 1981 to minimise its dependence on the US and deliveries there normally accounted for less than a quarter of its production. John Morgan, the company's export sales chief in the 1960s, maintains that Lyons laid down a policy of never allowing sales in any one market to rise above 25 to 30 per cent of the total. The UK was the only exception to that rule. This attitude appears to have been the product both of commercial sense and of an innate suspicion of the vagaries of the American market. "He was always terribly unhappy if one increased production for the United States," recalls Morgan. "With the E Type, I had the utmost difficulties in getting agreement to increase production in '65 and '66 and '67, when we had great possibilities to sell a large number of cars, but he would never go over the top."

Others saw the question of American sales in a different light. One senior manager of the time comments: "There's no question that throughout the period that Jaguar was an independent company, the demand for cars exceeded supply. In fact, in certain markets, particularly North America, history will record a huge missed opportunity."

By the end of the Leyland Cars period in the mid-1970s, the company was selling about 7,000 cars a year in America. That represented around 10 per cent of BL's annual sales in the US. MG sports cars accounted for the bulk of those sales, although the company did sell some Rover 3500 saloons in America. David Andrews was in charge of BL International at that time; he saw the distribution arrangements in the States as an obstacle in the way of improved profitability. "We didn't control the whole of the distribution," he explains. "We owned about half of it; the other half was in the hands of independents." Andrews maintains that the company was able to make money where it owned the distribution system, but where it went through an independent, the profit went to him.

One of the difficulties caused by the existence of independent distributors was that it was more difficult to make decisions. Whereas a manufacturer with a wholly owned distribution system can decide how to deal with currency fluctuations, for example, a company that is dealing through independent distributors might come under pressure from them. Added to that, the distributors may well have different ideas about how to run the business. As Jaguar's US chief Graham Whitehead puts it: "The interests of the manufacturer are not always adequately represented by an independent distributor. He may decide he has enough cars or needs to make some more money or doesn't want a particular model. We have assembly lines with so many cars coming off an hour and heading down to the boats. We need to work very closely with the supply end."

This question of control appears to have been an important factor influencing BL's decision to buy out the independents in America during the 1970s. It was not an easy task. Federal and state laws in the US make it virtually impossible for a manufacturer simply to sack his distributors, so agreements had to be reached with each independent. Andrews claims that the process cost BL £6 or £7 million, "one of the better buys". Certainly, had the task been attempted in the early 1980s, it would have been much more expensive, even if the distributors had been prepared to sell. By the end of the 1970s, the process was complete, and BL controlled distribution in the US through its subsidiary in Leonia, New Jersey.

During these and subsequent years, it seems that several approaches were made by individuals and companies interested in buying out the distribution. One of these was John DeLorean. At one time DeLorean had been an executive of General Motors, with a good chance of ultimately becoming president. In 1973, however, he left and started his own company, the John Z. DeLorean Corporation. He set about raising capital to begin manufacturing a sports car, and eventually persuaded the British government to put up a package of grants and loans worth a total of $97 million (£50 million). A factory was built in Belfast and production started in 1981. The company was never financially sound, but the government was persuaded to put still more money into the venture. Just over 5,000 cars had been built by February 1982, when a receiver was called in. By that time £97 million had been provided by the government.

Some time before the venture went bust, however, a meeting was held in New York between DeLorean and several BL directors to discuss the possibility of DeLorean buying BL's North American distribution system. He was turned down, but then approached Graham Whitehead with a different proposition. "We had quite a good parts distribution system," explains Whitehead. "John and his gang turned up to discuss whether we could warehouse his parts and distribute them for him in the US." This idea was also rejected. Soon after that meeting, the future of BL's American operation was placed in jeopardy by the closure of the MG factory at Abingdon, near Oxford.

At that time, around three quarters of MG sports cars were sold in the US, so the marque was more vulnerable than most to dollar movements. As the pound strengthened against the US currency, life became steadily more difficult for those selling MGs in America. "Our best customers," Andrews says, "were young professional women, graduates and guys working for themselves who bought sports cars. It was the m/s, miss market; female yuppies I suppose." Andrews maintains that the strong pound, and consequent substantial price rises, caused this market to fall away. "They'd spend $4,000 or $5,000 on a car, but they couldn't afford $7,000 or $8,000, so the market just went," he says. In his book *Back from the Brink*, Sir Michael Edwardes maintains that MG was losing £26 million a year by the end of the 1970s, £900 on every car sold in the USA. Although the main cause was the fact that the exchange rate had risen to nearly two dollars to the pound, there was no prospect of the situation easing in the near future. In September 1979, BL announced that MG was to close.

For the American dealers, the timing could hardly have been crueller. Two hundred of them were actually in Britain, celebrating 50 years of MG, when the bombshell was dropped. It fell to David Andrews to make the announcement at the final dinner of the trip, in what he recalls, surely without exaggeration, as "one of the more difficult speeches I had to make". The reaction was fierce; dealers threatened to march down Whitehall to present a petition to the Prime Minister at 10 Downing Street, and to send delegations to Parliament.

MG was regarded with great affection in both Britain and the US, but the more important factor from the American dealers' point of view was that it represented the bulk of their business. Without MG, all they had to sell was the Triumph TR7, which had never achieved much popularity and the construction quality of which was appalling; the Rover 3500, which had also failed to catch on; and the Jaguars, sales of which were the lowest for many years. The sales slump was caused not only by poor quality but also, according to many insiders, by supply shortages resulting from the crisis at the Castle Bromwich paint plant. Whitehead recalls that in the months after the MG closure, BL had "some difficulty in keeping the dealer body together".

There was nothing to offer them but promises.

When Egan joined Jaguar a little later, he had to convince the dealers that there was a future for them and the company – no mean task, given that fewer than 3,000 cars a year were being shipped to the US to be sold through about 240 dealers. Car dealers are geared to making profits, and the profit to be made by selling an average of one Jaguar a month was insufficient to keep them in business. The temptation to drop Jaguar in favour of another franchise must have been considerable. The cars, at that time, were unreliable, badly finished and thirsty and the US had suffered a fuel crisis in 1979. The word went round among the customers that, if one wanted a Jaguar, it was necessary to buy two: one to use while the other was being repaired.

It might seem surprising that BL wanted to retain any presence in America at all, yet it never had much alternative. By hanging on to the dealer network and by maintaining an office there, the company would at least avoid the enormous costs of starting up from cold again later. That would have been necessary because, if Jaguar was to have any future, it needed the US market. But perhaps more important was the fact that the company would have saved very little by pulling out. It would still have had to provide parts and service to owners of Jaguars, MGs, Rovers and Marinas (which were sold there for a while), and somebody would have had to be hired to do that. It would also have needed someone to handle the litigation that seems to be an integral part of American corporate life. All these considerations, combined with the indemnities that would have been paid if the dealer network had been wound up, meant that, commercially, it made sense to retain an American operation.

Egan was convinced that a turn round could be achieved and, when it happened, he would need dealers. The one thing that he had on his side was the fact that people liked Jaguars. The cars were still aesthetically attractive to customers and so it was clear that if quality could be improved the market would be there. In the summer of 1981, American dealers were brought to Britain for a conference. They were shown around the factory and there was a presentation of the new cars, including a brief glimpse of the XJ40, which would not be launched in the US for more than six years. A dinner was organised for the group at Warwick Castle with all the pomp and pageantry that could be mustered. "It was all designed to show them Britain at its traditional best," one manager comments. "It was a typical Jaguar family affair and its aim was to get them to stay with us." Another recalls: "It was absolute, total emotion," he says. "We hadn't got anything else. You couldn't stand up with some magic five-year plan. It was all, are you with us or aren't you? It was pure emotion and hype. There wasn't a dry eye left in the house and it worked."

The event was remarkably effective in raising dealers' morale; at last, it seemed, there was someone at Jaguar who cared about their difficulties. Until then, they had felt that their complaints about the quality of the cars were ignored. As each new model year car was introduced, the same faults continued to occur. The message of hope was relayed to the sales managers and general managers in meetings throughout the US, where Egan repeated his commitment to turn the company around. As Tony Cusmano, general manager of Rallye Motors in New Jersey explains: "I felt that there was someone on our side who was going to fight to put these cars together the right way and there was a big improvement in that, a big, big improvement."

Egan was aware of both the risks and the opportunities. "The danger, of course, was that the dealers would lose interest in the company," he says. "A few months earlier, BL had taken Triumph away, it'd taken Rover away, it'd taken MG away and would we have a network at all? But the opportunity was that, for the moment, dealers had nothing else to sell, and they did put their hearts and souls into it." Egan traded on the loyalty that many dealers had built up over the years. Cusmano says: "When you have something that you've built up, little by little; you've seen it grow, just like a child, you don't want to give it up. You always have the feeling and the hope that something's going to happen. We felt, something's got to happen sooner or later. We just fought like everybody else to hold on, pay the bills, and hoped that Jaguar was going to do something."

In many cases, the dealers had no option. One explains that he did think about taking other franchises. "Sure we looked around," he says. "But there was no one to get. We couldn't get any other franchises at that time. So we just did everything we could to keep the business going." Slowly, the drive for better quality and reliability began to show results, and word started to spread. Jaguars began to be seen as better cars and the process of rebuilding the company's reputation was aided by chat on the cocktail circuits of the East and West coasts.

The company's image was helped by the efforts of the Group 44 racing team. Group 44 had been racing Jaguars on US tracks with considerable success since the mid-1970s and had been supported by BL's North American company. As sales fell in the States, however, the funds for racing were cut, although Group 44 continued to compete. By 1980, it was in difficulties but an appeal to Jaguar for funds met with a friendly reception. Group

44's founder, Bob Tulius persuaded Egan that a successful racing programme in the US would help the company's revival. Egan agreed and Tony Ball authorised the expenditure from BLEO's promotional budgets. The result was the Jaguar XJR-5, an outright racing car designed and built in America using a Jaguar V12 engine. The XJR-5 competed in the International Motor Sports Association championship and even made an appearance at Le Mans, although success in that race was to elude the company until 1988.

In 1982, Jaguar's improving quality and enhanced image began to lift sales, in the US as elsewhere. This was helped by a change in the introduction of new model year cars. In the past, Jaguar had never got to grips with the cyclical nature of the new car market in the US, where the most important sales months are October to December. The company had consistently failed to have enough new model year cars in America ready to catch this peak market. But in 1981, the new models were delivered in time. There are differing accounts of how that happened. Some Jaguar people say the 1981 model year cars – which should have been introduced in late 1980 – were delayed and had not been long on the assembly lines when the American dealers visited the factory in July 1981. "We were five months late with the '81 model year," one executive explains, "so we missed a bit out and made it in the 1982 car. Since then, we've kept the model year spot on time." Others maintain that the '81 model year cars were deliberately missed out through "pragmatic management". However the change occurred it helped revive Jaguar's fortunes in the US.

Egan, however, insists that the crucial factor affecting sales performance in America was the transfer of responsibility for North American operations from BLEO to Jaguar during 1982. "From then on, we were able to treat our major market as part of the company rather than have any in-fighting with another organisation." (This is a reference to his battles with BLEO before the transfer.)

As the American dealers began to achieve higher sales, however, they thought they perceived a new threat on the horizon. Rumours began to circulate about a replacement for the XJ6 and

XJ12. "We were hoping they would stay with the old body style," Cusmano says, "and just improve on the engineering factors." His fear, shared by others in America, was that the styling of the new car would be dramatically different.

That was to be expected, because the American dealers had only recently begun to receive well built Series IIIs in numbers that allowed them to rebuild their businesses. In effect, the Series III was a new car in the US, and it was already to be replaced. The tendency over the previous few years to move towards a more "European", almost utilitarian, interior styling in XJ40 had fuelled their forebodings. The impact of drastic design changes would have been far greater in the US than elsewhere, if only because about half of American Jaguar drivers are women. Many come to Jaguars from Cadillacs and, according to American dealers, they find the transition easy. The smooth ride, soft seats and easy steering are all much closer to the Cadillac than to cars like the Mercedes or BMW. Jaguar salesmen have a better chance of persuading women to switch from Cadillacs than salesmen selling German cars. That was particularly important to the British company because it needed to convert owners of other cars, achieve "conquest sales", as the industry calls them, to stand a chance of increasing volumes.

Reaction to the new XJ40 saloon appears to have been mixed when it was finally launched in the US in the spring of 1987. Some dealers were delighted with it, but they also admit that it did not win universal approval from their customers. "A lot in the beginning did not like the style," one dealer recalls. "Then, after a few of them had gotten on the road and more people had seen them, they came around. You don't hear any more criticism of the new style now. Some of the older customers still have the old-style Jaguar and they still love it, but the new style is growing on them."

Fluctuating exchange rates have a crucial impact on Jaguar's fortunes, whatever the style. An exchange rate of over $2 to the pound had helped to precipitate the closure of MG. As one executive puts it: "There's no way you can make money in the States at $2.40 to the pound." However, the pound fell back against the dollar throughout the early 1980s and in February

1985 the rate stood at $1.10 to the pound. Jaguar picked up a tremendous windfall profits as a result. But by the time the XJ40 was launched in America, the pound was rising. This time, Jaguar was said to be less concerned because its main competition was from German manufacturers. If anything, they were even worse hit by the weak dollar than the British company.

Jaguar has, however, taken action to ensure that it does not suffer MG's fate (see Chapter 8). This is essential, since America is becoming almost as important to Jaguar as it once was to MG. At one time, it took 75 per cent of all MGs produced. It now takes over 50 per cent of Jaguars. Whether this is a calculated risk to improve profits while the company builds up sales in other markets, or whether the market opportunity has simply been grasped in a way that Lyons would never have allowed is not clear. Whatever the reason, it leaves the company in a vulnerable position. That said, Jaguar deserves the greatest credit for the progress it has achieved in America. Between 1980 and 1986, sales to the US increased eight-fold, from just under 3,000 units to well over 24,000. That is a remarkable record by anybody's standards.

CHAPTER 7

Spreading the Word

One of the key functions that John Egan fought from the beginning to bring under his direct control was sales and marketing, and although he had to wait until 1982 before he was allowed to install his own team at Browns Lane, he was provided with a dedicated group within BLEO. One member of that group was Peter Battam, who had been working on Jaguar advertising during the JRT years before 1980, along with John Chatham and Anne Greenwell. These three, between them, had a total of £200,000 a year to spend on Jaguar advertising. When Egan began demanding that someone be given responsibility for Jaguar within BLEO, Battam and Greenwell were again allocated to the task, although they continued to work out of the BLEO offices at Bickenhill on the outskirts of Birmingham.

They felt isolated. "We had our little office area at Bickenhill," Battam recalls, "and we were the Jaguar types and we weren't actually part of it any more. We just happened to live there." Within a short time, however, Battam began to spend most of his working hours at Browns Lane, usually in Egan's office, planning the publicity drive. The budgets, however, were still controlled by BLEO. The 1981 business plan, prepared in November 1980, allocated £1.5 million to advertise the whole Jaguar and Daimler range. This was less than BLEO planned to spend on either the Metro or the Ital or the Triumph Acclaim, which was due for launch later that year. The plan did, however, highlight the fact that "Jaguar/Daimler saloons are no longer considered to be value for money products compared to competitive models from Mercedes and BMW. This situation has been brought about by supply constrained premium pricing in recent years." The plan called for an increase in Jaguar and Daimler prices of no more than 3 per cent in July 1981.

Towards the end of December, 1980, in response to abysmal sales, BLEO staff put together a set of recommendations, including price cuts and a programme of advertising and promotional activities costing a total of £2.6 million. Poor quality and price-loading had led to large stocks of unsold cars which, at this point, were available only in three colours. Facelifted XJ6 and XJ12 models were expected in June 1981; there would be significant specification changes along with the introduction of the new high efficiency V12 engine. This was seen as an opportunity to bring Jaguar prices back into line, and certainly a more aggressive attitude to pricing was required. The proposals were rejected by Jaguar.

Three months later, after the BL board meeting that had discussed the closure of Browns Lane, the document was resurrected. Parts of it were accepted and a big advertising push began. An important purpose of this campaign was to tell customers that the quality of the cars was improving. As Battam puts it: "The whole thing, at that time, was to rekindle interest in the product; to say there was a new management regime; to say that quality was improving. We were trying to re-awaken interest and support the dealers."

For the first and only time, Jaguar advertised its products on television. (Individual dealers were to be encouraged to use television later.) Viewers were invited to test drive a Jaguar and see how much better the product was. "We booked air time around *News at Ten*," Battam explains. "At the end of the commercial, we invited people to call a special telephone number to book a test drive." A team of girls sat by the telephones until the early hours. It is rumoured that they received only three telephone calls, all of them abusive. As a stimulus to test drives, the commercial did not work. Battam insists, however, that it did have a beneficial effect. "It was the first time that any luxury car manufacturer had gone on television. It did a lot in terms of reawakening interest in Jaguar."

The television commercial was accompanied by press advertising and evening promotions based in dealers' showrooms. These events included a presentation of the company's past by the late Andrew Whyte, a leading authority on Jaguar's history, and finished with a film. In earlier years, BL had bought the rights to a film in which James Coburn, the American actor, talked about the Le Mans 24 hour race and about the Jaguar C and D Type cars that had repeatedly won it in the 1950s. This was edited down to produce a 20-minute film that rounded the evening off.

Perhaps the most important aspect of these events was that Jaguar directors took part in them. Mike Beasley, who was to become deputy managing director, says: "To have a customer who's absolutely fed up with his car telling you so, brings home that it is the customer who counts. It was an extremely valuable exercise, not just selling cars, which we did and we needed to do, desperately, but it brought home that we had made a lot of customers unhappy and that we'd got a long way to go." The success of these evenings led the publicity team to think about other ways of talking directly to customers.

One of the most surprising was alluded to in the 1981 business plan. Battam had an ambition at the time to create what he describes as "the Martini" image for Jaguar. A perfect opportunity arose when he was approached by a company called Turbeau, which had been set up to develop the V12 Jaguar engine for marine use. As part of the development programme, twin turbo chargers were fitted and two engines were installed in an offshore racing boat. The objective was to prove that the Jaguar engine was fast and reliable and then to sell the engines to other power-boat racers.

Offshore racing fitted Battam's idea of the "Martini image" perfectly, and Jaguar gave Turbeau engineering assistance to develop the engines. "It was the only thing we were doing in those days that was fast and glamorous," Battam recalls. "We used to hang dealer promotions on the power-boat racing. We'd hire a luxury boat, put 40 customers on it, take them out on the ocean, have a beautiful lunch on board, a few drinks and bob about on the briny watching the power boats." The association with offshore racing went sour some time later, when a company run by one of the partners in Turbeau ran into difficulties. The boat had, by now, been signwritten with the Jaguar logo and featured in a television programme about the financial affairs of this company. As a result, Jaguar pulled out of offshore power-boat racing.

Bill Bonner had been involved in the project through his south coast company, Bonner Marine. He continued developing the V12 to the point at which it was claimed to deliver 800 brake horse-power. In July 1983, Bonner won his class in the Cancer Research Race off Poole in his boat *Supercat*. Colin Gervaise Brazier had installed two of the engines in his boat *Goldrush*, and he won that year's Fowey Offshore Peter Stuyvesant Trophy. During 1984, Gervaise Brazier won several races outright, having renamed his boat *The Legend*, reflecting the Jaguar advertising theme of that year. The programme was cancelled at the end of 1984, owing to alleged irregularities in Jaguar's procurement area involving parts for the power-boats.

Battam recalls the period with pleasure. "You had two engines, so you had four six-inch diameter exhaust stacks coming out of the back of the boat," he says. "Glorious sound. To drive the boat was frightening. It was 42 feet long, and when you stand in the cockpit, it was just decking. You wind the throttles open and all you can hear is the turbochargers. Five and a quarter tons just leaps out of the water because all it does is steam along on the step plates at the back. When you get to about 80 miles an hour, she's flat, so you can see where you're going. Bouncing along at 80, 90, 100 miles an hour over eight-foot holes in the ocean is something else."

Motor sport obviously had to be considered as an image builder. Jaguar gained worldwide publicity with its Le Mans victories. But the company had officially withdrawn from racing in 1956. Jaguars were seen again at the race tracks, albeit briefly, in 1977 when the ill conceived Big Cat racing programme was run by Broadspeed Engineering, of Southam, Warwickshire. These racing XJ 5.3Cs were enormously popular with the fans, but failed to achieve much success. But Ford had used motor sport to enhance its attraction for younger motorists and it seemed reasonable to expect that Jaguar could do the same, provided it could win. The company had supported the Group 44 cars that raced in the US for some years, but that had little publicity value in Europe.

In March, 1983, the company announced that it was to sponsor a team of two XJ-Ss in that year's European Touring Car championship. The cars would be prepared and raced by Tom Walkinshaw Racing (TWR), based near Banbury, Oxfordshire. Co-sponsored by Motul Oil, the team was destined to become runners-up to BMW in 1983. Explaining the reason for the return to the motor racing circuits in the first issue of *Jaguar Racing Review*, which appears at every race meeting where the company competes, Jim Randle wrote: "The new regulations called Group A mean that there is an international category in Europe for cars bearing a close relationship to those the customer can go out and buy for everyday use." He pointed out that the overall shape of the cars could not be changed, so people could see recognisable cars racing.

The main competition was the BMW 635CSi, which was able to run lighter because of the way the regulations were drafted. Fuel tank capacity was limited to 120 litres, which meant that the Jaguars had to make two fuelling stops in the average race while the BMWs could manage on one. Under the circumstances, to win second place in the first year of competition in the championship was remarkable.

But 1984 proved to be even better. Tom Walkinshaw became European Touring Car champion, the first British driver to achieve that distinction in over 20 years. In April the following year, Jaguar announced that TWR was to build a new endurance race car, the XJR-6, to compete in the World Sports-Prototype Championship series. This car won its first victory in 1986. In the few years since its reappearance on motor racing circuits, Jaguar has achieved some remarkable successes. Perhaps the most important of these came on June 12, 1988, when a Jaguar again crossed the finishing line in first place at Le Mans, after a gap of 31 years.

Power-boats and motor racing fitted the Jaguar image, but they were quite alien to Daimler. Here, a different approach was needed. Several famous artists were invited to produce their image of the marque, in their own medium, for an advertising campaign. These were known as the "masterpiece" advertisements; various originals can still be seen at Browns Lane. Building on this theme, John Maries who had, by now, replaced Anne Greenwell in the sales and marketing team, developed the idea of Daimler musical evenings.

They hired a group of young professional musicians just starting out on their careers. The ensemble was taken to various stately homes and country houses where the local dealer would entertain invited guests. The music would last for an hour and a half and be followed by a buffet supper. "It was always black tie," Battam explains. "They were very superior evenings, in keeping with Daimler, whereas with Jaguar, everybody rushed about with noisy engines of some sort or another." The musical evenings were run for three years and did generate orders. Artists' foibles had to be accommodated of course. The pianist insisted on a Steinway piano, which had to be transported around the country. On one occasion there was anguish when the instrument became jammed on the stairs of Cardiff Castle on the way to the library.

The biggest problem in any promotional campaign such as this is that of finding suitable venues for events, particularly when activities like clay pigeon shooting and point-to-point are included. To overcome this difficulty, an ingenious vehicle called the "Big Rig" was designed and built. The basis of the Big Rig is an articulated truck that opens out to form a covered octagonal area with a turntable in the middle for displaying cars. Space for up to 160 people can be provided in this way. "That gave us our own catering facility anywhere we wanted to take it," Battam explains. "It starts its working life each year in about April and finishes at the end of October." Big Rig was so successful that it was joined by other promotional equipment which is used at motor racing meetings, county shows, exhibitions and dealer showroom events.

Over the years, a sophisticated promotional programme has been developed that now accounts for around half of the marketing budget. Battam estimates that the company invites around 40,000 potential customers to events in the course of a year. "We still find that talking to dealers and customers is ultimately the best way of selling luxury motor cars," he says. Such activities have steadily added to the workload of the small publicity team, even though it has grown in numbers since 1980. The most visible of these in the home market is the bi-annual British motor show.

Jaguars and Daimlers had been displayed alongside volume cars since the beginning of Leyland Cars. In 1981, the company once again had its own stand, and it was decided that this should be closed, with barriers around it. Battam maintains that a closed stand, with carefully briefed staff, gives people a better chance to see the cars and learn something of them. He admits that valued customers occasionally have to queue to enter the stand. There seems little doubt that one reason for adopting this approach is that it helps to enhance the company's "exclusive" image.

As efforts to improve product quality and company image made progress, people in quite different lines of business began to see value in the Jaguar name. One of these was Kevin Boocock, then managing director of Salisbury Handbags. He had recently bought an XJ-S and was very impressed with it. He telephoned Egan and suggested that a Jaguar Collection of merchandise should be designed. Work progressed on the idea and Battam maintains that the design and quality of the goods assembled was excellent. According to him, it could have been a British equivalent to Gucci, but ultimately the collaboration with Boocock was terminated. "The whole thing suddenly stopped," Battam says, "so the Collection never really got off the ground." It still exists, but appears to have lost its way, and now includes a motley range of goods from model cars to a silver plated drinks decanters and expensive luggage. It represents a missed opportunity.

The biggest success for the publicity department far outweighs this, however, because it affects the image of every Jaguar dealer in Britain. One of the difficulties faced by all car manufacturers and importers is that they do not control their dealers' marketing efforts. In most cases, dealers seem not to understand what marketing involves and do little more than take advertising space in local newspapers and magazines, the quality of which in any case varies enormously. They fail to sell as many cars as they could because they do not go out looking for business. The salesmen tend to sit in their showrooms and wait for the customers to come to them. Dealers' profitability is consequently lower than it should be. If they are not making adequate profits, they cannot invest in improved facilities and that affects customers' perceptions of both the dealer and the manufacturer.

By the beginning of 1983, the first steps were being taken to restructure the Jaguar dealer network. The primary objective was to appoint more efficient and professional dealers and it was obviously necessary to find ways of helping them improve their marketing. Battam had already gained some experience of how to do that during his years with Leyland Cars and BLEO. One of his colleagues from that time, Ray Underwood, had left BL to join the Birmingham advertising agency RTA. Underwood had been around the car business for many years. He had worked for a dealer in Cambridge, spent two and a half years in Austin-Morris regional sales offices, and then several more working in sales promotions for Leyland Cars and BLEO. Underwood knew the business and more important, he understood the dealers. Battam met him at RTA's offices one afternoon early in 1983 to discuss the question of how to make the network more professional in its marketing approach. Underwood points out that much advertising at the time was of miserable quality. One of the battles in the early days was against dealers who advertised cars at discounted prices. It was the "One only, never a better time to buy . . ." brand of advertising that they wanted to stamp out.

Battam outlined Jaguar's aspirations for the future, and Underwood admits to having been a little sceptical at the start. "I couldn't help feeling I'd seen it all before," he recalls. Underwood knew that the BL dealers were very powerful and if they wanted to kill a programme they could. There had been many instances of that happening over the years. As Battam talked, however, Underwood began to realise that this time, the story could be different. He then met Roger Putnam, Jaguar's sales operations director, was impressed by what he had to say and took a brief. At that time, nothing had been published about the franchise development fund or about minimum standards, but Underwood was told what would be covered. "The idea was to put in consistent programmes, not ones that were going to change every year," he says.

It was clear to Underwood that far more was involved than simply local dealer advertising. He attempted to create a programme that would help to change dealers' approach to selling Jaguars and Daimlers. It was from that thought that the programme's name emerged. "I thought if we called it the Jaguar dealer co-operative advertising service, it would be no different to anything else," he says. "I didn't think it was about advertising, because plonking ads in the local paper every week is not going to bring people back to the fold. I thought contact was what it was all about. It was about making contact with prime prospects, potential prospects, no more than that." When Contact was launched, it was presented in a dark green box containing all the basic information about the service, along with sample advertisements and advice on how to adopt an effective marketing approach. Dealers were alerted to the existence of the programme through a mock "tablet of stone" set in clear perspex. On one side, this carried Jaguar's advertising code of practice and on the other, information about the service. Little in Contact was entirely new. It contained a code of practice that covered dealers' advertising; it offered help with choosing the right media for advertising; it provided materials that could be used to make up advertisements. On the face of it, there was no reason why Contact should work when similar programmes from other manufacturers had not. What set it apart, however, was that it had total commitment from Egan down. Underwood emphasises that Contact provides a strategy rather than short-term solutions to specific problems. Gradually, dealers grasped the message and began to use the strategy.

Over the following years, other activities were added. A television commercial to promote the franchise was developed. This was used on Channel 4 by around a third of the dealers. "It was a kit commercial," says Underwood. "Each time we did it, we rejigged it with a unique voice-over, so that it was the dealer's own commercial. Most dealer launches through '85 and '86 were on television." Now, Jaguar insists that dealers spend a specified amount on marketing for each car they sell. This ruling was included in minimum standards in 1984, when it was laid down that £200 had to be spent on marketing for each car sold. Dealers have complete flexibility in how the money is spent, as long as it goes on marketing activities.

One of the most important advances of recent years has involved used cars. At one time, many dealers either ignored used cars or failed to run their used car sales departments properly. Jaguar dealers were not unusual in this. Many car manufacturers spend a great deal of time trying to persuade dealers to adopt a more professional attitude to used cars. Not only does failure to sell used cars at retail reduce the profitability of the dealership; it also means that the manufacturer has no control over the value of used cars. It is important for a company to achieve good used-car prices because one of the factors affecting car purchasing decisions is the likely value of the vehicle in 12 months' or two years' time. It if depreciates too much, people will turn to other makes. A used car programme was implemented, and RTA identified as a primary need a special Jaguar section in the *Sunday Times*. Underwood describes the used car section of that newspaper as ". . . the focal point for buying a luxury used car if you don't go to your local dealership".

The task was not easy, because most dealers saw the *Sunday Times* as being far too expensive. RTA, however, negotiated a deal with the newspaper and then suggested that the dealers should try it. For the dealers, this was a useful development, although all of their advertisements have to go through Contact. It means that the copy can be vetted before it appears. Jaguar has clearly defined rules governing what a dealer can and cannot do in terms of advertising. One of those dictates that a used demonstrator must be advertised as "price on application". The main reason for this is said to be to avoid giving the impression that any Jaguar is being dropped quickly, possibly because the owner did not like it. However, it is also thought that the rule was intended partly to stamp out the inevitable black market in the XJ40 when it began to be advertised, by stopping dealers from advertising them overtly.

Underwood stresses that Contact is more than a set of rules and a box of advertisements. "It's the culture, it's the concept, it's the attitude," he says, pointing out that it has been translated into other European markets successfully. The concept has played an important part in Jaguar's revival, as has the publicity programme as a whole. There would have been little point in achieving improved quality standards if the company had not bothered to tell potential customers about it. And even if, as Battam maintains, it was not necessary to advertise XJ40 throughout 1987 (see chapter 10), the company has continued to sharpen its presence and profile through promotional activities.

CHAPTER 8
Returning to Profit

Many have claimed that Jaguar has always been profitable, and it is true that profits were recorded for every year between the company's formation and its takeover by BMC. From 1968 to 1979, however, Jaguar's financial performance was inextricably bound into BL's overall figures, so no one can prove that the company was profitable at that time. Perhaps the most reliable analysis is provided by John Edwards who took over as financial director in 1980. In trying to reconstruct the accounts for the missing years, as part of the preparations for Jaguar's privatisation, he talked to Mike Lane, who had been Jaguar's chief accountant. Lane was adamant that Jaguar made profits up to 1974. After that point, it is more difficult to be sure although Edwards is convinced that the company was still profitable. "From Geoffrey Robinson's days on, you have to recreate the accounts," he says. "But based on the volumes [of sales] and the exchange rates and the workforce they'd got, they must have returned profits." He admits that they were not particularly big. "The best I saw was '75, about £15 million," he explains. "In '74 it was about £12 million and we spent about £8 million on the XJ-S tooling, but they weren't big numbers. In the early 1970s it was around £10 million."

That changed in 1979, when the company lost, Edwards estimates, "between £40 and £50 million". The loss was £47 million in 1980 and £32 million in 1981. From 1979 to 1981, therefore, the company lost between £119 million and £129 million. The first task facing the new management was to stem the flow of money out of the company. Edwards had to establish where the money was flowing from.

The losses were caused by several factors. Jaguar was geared up to produce around 30,000 cars a year. It needed to produce and sell that number in order to cover its overheads. However, the new paint plant at Castle Bromwich made it impossible to do so, partly because it did not achieve the required levels of production, partly because many bodies were rejected by Jaguar inspectors. In 1979, the company had produced only 14,000 cars. In addition, stock levels in the UK were too high. That was a drain on resources because unsold cars have to be financed by the company, and that involves interest payments. The high level of stocks was made worse by the fact that for 18 months or so, because of the troubles at the paint plant, cars were all finished in one of three colours, white, yellow or red. It is generally agreed that the only acceptable colour was white.

The strength of sterling was another burden. In 1980, Jaguar would export over 60 per cent of its production with the pound at an average of $2.33. The unfavourable exchange rate had several causes. The Conservatives had been returned to power in the 1979 general election. Britain's trading partners were impressed by the public statements of the new government and the pound rose as a result. North Sea oil, with its colossal contribution to the UK balance of payments, gave the process further impetus. Michael Edwardes was quoted at the time as saying that, if that was what North Sea oil did for the country, the stuff should be left in the ground! Interest rates in Britain were also high. All these factors, combined with a general loss of confidence in the US, drove the pound up.

The idea that a strong pound was bad for Britain was not then fashionable. A strong body of opinion, however, holds that the strength of the pound wiped out much of UK industry. Its effect at Jaguar was that the company earned less from overseas sales. The company's 1984 offer for sale document illustrated the potency of fluctuating exchange rates. A table showed the operating profit or loss that could have been expected during 1983, had the only change been in the sterling/dollar exchange rate. The average for that year was $1.52 to the pound and the company made a profit of £51 million. Had the pound fallen to only $1.20, Jaguar could have made around £112 million. On the other hand, at $2 to the pound, there would have been a loss of £5 million.

(Obviously, had the pound risen to that level, action would have been taken to limit the damage.)

But there was nothing that the company could do directly to affect exchange rates. Michael Edwardes made representations to government but was, apparently, unable to persuade it that an overvalued pound damaged industry as a whole and BL in particular. The traditional view of a high pound was that the penalties suffered in export markets were offset by cheaper imports of raw materials. In Jaguar's case, however, this quid pro quo did not operate. Most of the company's raw materials were bought in Britain and most of its components were made by British companies. So there was no saving on purchasing to set against the losses on overseas sales.

John Edwards's immediate problem when he arrived at Jaguar was to find out exactly what state the company's finances were in. "Nobody knew quite how bad they were," he says. "Certainly the financial forecasting that was done at the time was too optimistic." A loss of about £20 million for that year had been predicted. The reality was over twice that. To bring the losses under control and begin to reduce them, it was necessary to cut the company's overheads and the numbers of cars held in stock and, in the longer term, make Jaguar more efficient. This, along with the drive to improve quality, had absolute priority. Late in 1980, the production lines were stopped for three weeks. This was aimed, primarily, at providing a breathing space to sort out the paint problems, but it also reduced the stock levels. Edwards maintains that stock inventories were cut by half in the last six months of 1980.

The workforce was drastically reduced. In 1980, Jaguar employed over 10,000 people, and produced 1.4 cars per employee per year. By mid-1981, the number of employees had been reduced to just under 8,000. This was the point at which the American dealers were persuaded to throw their weight behind the new management. That, combined with improving quality and reliability, meant an increased demand for the cars, so the workforce was increased again to a little over 8,000. By now, however, the company was building 3.4 cars per year per employee.

Mid-1981 was, in fact, a particularly good time for Jaguar: the exchange rate was also moving in the right direction. By July, it was down to around $1.87 to the pound and falling. Added to that, the new HE V12 engine was announced for the XJ-S and the XJ12, giving a new lease of life to these profitable cars. The XJ-S was also given a revised interior and the prices of the whole range were cut by an average of 6 per cent. Premium pricing by BL over the preceding years meant that Jaguars were no longer seen as good value for money when measured against the products of competitors such as Mercedes-Benz – and certainly not when the build quality of the Mercedes and the Jaguar were compared.

The turning-point for Jaguar came, then, in 1981. Edwards recalls the year as falling into two distinct halves. The first was as bad as 1980, which would have meant a loss of around £23 million for the half year. The second half he describes as ". . . a distinct improvement", since the company ended the year with a loss of just under £32 million. By 1982, things were moving strongly in Jaguar's favour. Quality improvements were starting to come through. A sales target of 6,000 cars was set for the US, but American dealers in fact sold 10,000. That rose to 16,000 in 1983 and, with a stronger dollar, money flowed into Jaguar at a gratifying rate. A £15 million profit was recorded in 1982 – not enormous, but at least it was a move in the right direction. By this time, Jaguar was running its own finance department and its own treasury operation.

The acquisition of treasury was particularly important because that is the department that looks after the conversion of overseas currencies into sterling, among other things. Once he had control there, Edwards was able to begin taking action to offset some of the effects of currency fluctuations. This process, known as hedging, was seen as particularly important, since around 75 per cent of Jaguar's revenue was in overseas currencies at that time. Hedging makes possible a greater degree of planning, because it enables the company accurately to forecast overseas incomes in sterling instead of having to accept whatever exchange rates apply when the money comes in. Late in 1984, Jaguar began to take out forward exchange contracts on dollars. These are contracts with one of the major banks to sell the dollars the company expects to receive at a pre-determined price. Jaguar does this only on dollar receipts and only for 75 per cent of those. Normally, it is done on a 12-month rolling basis, though Edwards says that at the end of 1984 and early in 1985, when the dollar was very strong, two years' cover was taken out, to obtain maximum advantage.

Edwards stresses that hedging is an important management instrument used to increase Jaguar's profits. "You've got predictability. You've got stability within the business, because most of the costs are in sterling," he says. "Nearly all the capital expenditure is sterling, so I've got to have a lot of sterling to pay the bills. I need to take the uncertainty out of not knowing what the exchange rate is on a day to day basis. This way, I lock in profit. I know what it is and I can plan." Hedging, then reduced Jaguar's exposure to fluctuating exchange rates.

Another urgent need was to reduce the costs of financing stock at the factory. A car manufacturer incurs interest charges through holding stock in two main ways: some cars cannot be delivered because they need rectification or because a component is lacking, and some are held at the factory because there are no orders to cover them. Better management largely dealt with the first problem, by ensuring that components were available when needed. Increased demand, particularly in the US, reduced stocks of finished cars. These two developments helped cash-flow considerably, but the possibilites were not yet exhausted.

Under normal circumstances, Jaguar claims to pay suppliers within 45 days. By 1986, it was taking around 56 days from delivery of the body panels to despatch of a finished car. Cars destined for the UK market are paid for as soon as they leave the factory, but the company might wait anything up to 30 days for payment for exported vehicles. So Jaguar has to finance finished stock for anything between 10 days and six weeks, depending on where it is to be sold and assuming that everything is operating at maximum efficiency. This was a dramatic improvement over earlier times, when it was not uncommon to have cars sitting at the factory for several months before they were despatched.

In manufacturing, the "just in time" concept was introduced, aimed at reducing the company's need to finance stocks of components. Where traditional methods involve a manufacturer taking deliveries of components from time to time and holding stocks of them, just in time methods rely on suppliers maintaining a steady stream of deliveries. In some cases, a manufacturer will hold enough components for only one shift. Obviously, this means that if a supplier lets it down, the assembly lines will grind to a halt more quickly, but many manufacturers have decided that the risks are worth the reduction in overheads.

Hand in hand with "just in time", went the drive to improve productivity. In 1980, the company had produced 1.4 cars per employee per year. By 1985, that had risen to 4 cars per employee per year. This was brought about partly by reducing the workforce in the early years. Just over 9,000 people were employed by Jaguar in the UK in 1980; in 1982 that was down to 7,500. Those who were left worked more efficiently and better use was made of resources, so that over the same period, production rose from 13,791 cars to 22,046.

The drive for increased productivity, along with the introduction of a new engine and a new car, required considerable investments in new plant and equipment. "To remain competitive," Edwards says, "we have to spend 8 to 10 per cent of net sales on capital expenditure and 5 per cent of sales on engineering and research and development."

The fact that the company has earned levels of profits that enable it to invest in the future is a direct result of management decisions taken since 1980. The dollar/pound exchange rate helped the process considerably, however. It remains to be seen whether Jaguar can continue to earn enough with the pound standing higher against the dollar.

CHAPTER 9
Going Public

Ken Edwards, who has been involved with Jaguar on and off since the 1960s and has been company secretary since the privatisation, knew that Jaguar was likely to be floated several years before it happened. At Jaguar-Rover-Triumph, he had been responsible for the business plan. "Every time I wrote the plan, it had in the front that the main aim was to get the company into a position where we could attract outside capital," he explains. Certainly Egan's view, from the beginning, was that the company should be privatised. "I was made aware of the gathering requirement of British Leyland to get outside funding from other sources," he says. "Now what that was going to mean was unclear, but those were the words that were being used. From my own point of view, I always saw it as being run as an independent company . . . I didn't see it as, long-term, a part of British Leyland."

There was a long and hard road to travel, however, before aspiration could become reality. The year before Egan arrived, huge losses had been posted, and it was not until the latter half of 1981 that the company began to make profits again. But by the end of 1982, it was beginning to look as if the improvement in the company's position was more than a flash in the pan. John Edwards recalls that discussions at the end of 1982 began to centre on the question of selling off at least one part of BL. Sir Michael Edwardes had left by that time. He had been replaced as chairman by Sir Austin Bide, with Ray Horrocks and David Andrews as chief executives, Horrocks responsible for cars and Andrews for trucks. Until then, it had been assumed that the first part of the company to be floated would be Land Rover, which had been earning profits for some years. Then Land Rover's fortunes took a dive, so attention turned, instead, to Jaguar.

"I wasn't party to the BL board's conversations," Edwards

explains, "but our understanding was that it had been given the task of privatising some part of BL before the next election." Margaret Thatcher's first government had been elected in May 1979 so, if that timetable was a serious proposal, it would have meant that a part of BL would have had to be floated by May 1984. That did not leave much time to establish a track record that would impress investors sufficiently to make them want to buy shares. In the event, the election took place in June 1983, and a Conservative government was again returned. The following December, pressure on BL was increased when Norman Lamont, the Minister of State for Industry, used a debate on the motor industry to announce that Jaguar would be sold during the coming year.

The company's potential for a stock market listing was considerably enhanced by a series of approaches that took place during 1982 and 1983. The first involved Ford, which suggested that it should act as importer and distributor for Jaguar in West Germany and North America. Ford, in the early 1980s, was looking for a prestige name to add to its stable, but it does not appear to have suggested a full takeover at this stage. Most of the discussions seem to have centred on the suggested European arrangements. The attraction for Jaguar was that it would gain a good dealer body in the biggest luxury car market in Europe: Germany. Egan says the idea was that Jaguar would produce a branded car for distribution through Ford outlets. It might have been called Daimler or it might have been Lanchester. Daimler was discounted as a possibility because of the obvious confusion with Daimler-Benz, but Ford researched the possibility of using the Lanchester name, according to Egan.

Lanchester was one of the earliest car manufacturers in Britain, had been acquired by Daimler and so had passed into Jaguar's ownership when William Lyons had bought Daimler. However, the Americans established that the name produced the wrong resonances in Germany. "The Lanchester was dismissed because they confused it with the Lancaster bomber and Burt Lancaster," Egan says. "They did some pretty good surveys and they dismissed both names." During negotiations, Neil Johnson, Jaguar's sales and marketing director, went to Germany to look at some of the Ford dealerships. He was not particularly impressed with what he saw, in terms of the ability to sell luxury cars, and concluded that Jaguar could do better in Germany itself. The idea of a link with Ford seems to have risen and died quickly, but not before it had an effect, both within BL and within Jaguar. "I think Ford did a service to us," Egan says, "because the fact that they were interested did at least mean that some people in BL took more interest in us, so they did some good for our morale."

Egan had been arguing fiercely with BLEO about the potential for Jaguar sales in the US. BLEO thought 2,500 was a realistic target for 1982. "Ford were quite adamant that 10,000 was what they'd be going for, or some bigger number, so it did tend to lend credence to the kind of ideas that we had as to what was possible," Egan says. There were dangers in the numbers being discussed, however. Ken Edwards points out that an extensive dealer network might have created a greater demand than Jaguar could meet. There was also the question of image. Ford products are mainstream, volume cars, so the deal that was being proposed would have flown in the face of the franchising policy that was evolving at Jaguar. This demanded a split from the Austin-Rover volume cars franchise and an increase in the number of Jaguar-only showrooms.

For John Morgan, Jaguar's director of continental European operations, there was another consideration: "We were leaving a company that was in difficulties anyway. It was another British company, and it would have been pretty mean to have gone to their direct competitors and given them a product that was just beginning to become valuable. BL had only had a year or two of gravy with it in 10 years. Really, it would have been unthinkable to have gone to a Ford distributor." In due course, Jaguar did change its arrangements in Germany, but, Morgan points out, "we managed to achieve what we did with no real damage to the network of either company." The Ford approach was turned down.

Ford was immediately followed by BMW. Discussions took place on two levels: at one stage, the German company was negotiating to take a controlling stake in Jaguar while also exploring the possibilities of collaboration on a small Jaguar, probably based on the BMW 5 Series floor pan. Chief engineer Jim Randle was heavily involved in the talks on a new car. "It was exploratory," he says. "However, we did disclose our future products to BMW and they disclosed theirs to us. We knew about their 7 Series and they knew about our XJ40." This could mean that discussions reached an advanced stage, for such a degree of trust between two rival companies is extraordinary. Neither the 7 Series BMW nor the XJ40 had been launched, and manufacturers habitually go to extreme lengths to keep new products secret. However, these discussions, too, came to nothing. Egan believes that the Jaguar management was already making too much demonstrable progress for BMW to be able to claim credit for turning the company round. Contrary to some claims, no proposed agreement between the two companies ever went to the government for approval.

By now, the Browns Lane team must have been getting used to approaches from putative suitors. Yet another appeared in 1983: General Motors. It cannot have come as a complete surprise. Like Ford, GM wanted a prestige name to add to its stable. Jaguar appears, however, to have been hostile to the idea of a GM takeover from the start, probably because it was increasingly confident of its ability to succeed on its own. GM's approach appears to have been friendly although senior Jaguar managers were extremely concerned about the implications. One insider says the prospect of a deal with GM was described within the company as being like an elephant and a mouse getting into a bath together. "Sooner or later, the elephant, no matter how kind he is, will crush the mouse." The affair ended when Egan explained to GM chief executive Roger Smith that the Jaguar management did not necessarily go with the company. Smith was enough of a realist to recognise that Jaguar without Egan and his team would not be the same as Jaguar with them.

One result of all this activity was to enhance the company's reputation and that of its management. That, in turn, helped to emphasise that Jaguar was now a realistic proposition for privatisation. From BL's point of view, of course, there was no sense in selling off the one part of the group that was beginning to make substantial profits. Commercial logic suggested that it should be retained in order, at the very least, that it should pay back the money that had been provided through BL for investment in new product development and facilities. In 1982, £2.1 million was paid back to BL, and during the following two years another £100.5 million. According to John Edwards, Jaguar made a substantial loss, probably £40 million to £50 million in 1979, and BL pumped £90.7 million into the company in 1980 and 1981. So BL retrieved a high proportion of the cash that it had provided. But in any case, government pressure on the BL board made it inevitable that Jaguar would return to the private sector.

The main question was when? BL maintained that XJ40 should be launched before the company was privatised. Its reasoning was that a new car is always a risk and it was inadvisable to float the company with a potential millstone around its neck. Now that XJ40 has been launched and is such a success, the suggestion that it could have failed might seem an absurdity, yet the history of the motor industry is littered with the wrecks of cars that their makers confidently expected to be winners. Until it appears in the market place and the public begins to buy it in substantial numbers, no car can be assumed to be a winner. (In the case of the XJ40, of course, the consequences of failure would have been catastrophic, since the XJ6 that it replaced represented around 80 per cent of Jaguar's business.)

The counter-argument from within Jaguar was that XJ40 was so far from being ready to launch that, if BL did not allow the engineers time to get it properly sorted out, there would be a two-fold failure: privatisation would be late and XJ40 would fail because of insufficient development time.

The arguments continued through the second half of 1983. In September, Coopers & Lybrand were brought in as auditors and reporting accountants; at the same time, John Edwards recalls having his first meeting with Trevor Swete and Robert Dutton of the merchant bank, Hill Samuel, which was to act as issuing house. The process of turning Jaguar back into a private sector, independent company had begun. Through December 1983 and the first three months of 1984, a first offer for sale document was drafted. The target date for privatisation was May 1984. The first draft was very different from the document that was eventually presented to potential investors. The original intention was for BL to retain 25 per cent of Jaguar. Ray Horrocks says that, in his view, there were strong commercial reasons for BL to retain a stake. He was concerned about the possibility that a company such as BMW or General Motors might build up a substantial holding in Jaguar and then make a bid for it; and he thought it was a good trade investment for BL.

In Jaguar's eyes, however, this was merely further proof that BL was unwilling to let go. Edwards says: "The feeling that we had was that the BL board was being pushed, and I assumed it was always by the government." The proposal for BL to retain a stake was put to the Department of Trade and Industry, which apparently accepted it. Jaguar had gone along with it because, in Edwards's words, "at least we'd be 75 per cent on our own". Then the deal was put forward for approval by the cabinet. The government took the view that the question of a trade investment for BL was not a consideration. It was committed to privatisation as a policy and it seems likely that for that reason it set its face against any sort of halfway house. It is believed both by Ray Horrocks and at Jaguar, that Margaret Thatcher herself vetoed the BL proposal. That left Horrocks's first concern, a possible takeover bid for Jaguar, unresolved. But the government had an answer to that: a "golden share".

The golden share, referred to in the official paperwork as the "special share", is held by the Secretary of State for Trade and Industry and allows the minister to block any attempted takeover or voluntary liquidation of the company. Apart from that, the golden share does not give its owner any more power over the running of the company than any other share. From Jaguar's point of view, it is an ideal arrangement, since the company is protected from damaging takeover battles until the golden share expires on December 31, 1990.

Originally, it seems, the government wanted the golden share to be a permanent part of the company's issued share capital. However, the merchant banks that were to underwrite the issue apparently told Norman Tebbit, then Secretary of State for Trade and Industry, that they would not proceed on those terms. Their argument was that, if the government were able to veto any moves that could lead to Jaguar's acquisition by another company, it would not be a true public company.

That decision took a while to filter back to Jaguar, and it was not until May 1984 that work began on a revised offer for sale. Now that the company was to be separated entirely from BL, several relationships had to be redefined. "We worked in May and June to reorganise the company," John Edwards says. "We put a lot of legal contracts in place to separate our business in commercial terms from the rest of BL. In other words, the panels supply, parts supply and the Istel relationship." Istel was the computer systems house at that time owned by BL. Personnel and administration, sales and marketing, public relations and finance had already been brought back into Jaguar. "We gradually built up a company with all the supports," Horrocks says. "We agreed areas where Jaguar would buy a service, like pensions, for instance, from BL. We agreed the parts arrangement and we talked about the Coventry warehouse. We set out to make the thing as free standing as was sensible." Sales and marketing director Neil Johnson was involved in negotiating many of the details, "for example, the contract with Unipart, the contracts with Austin-Rover over distribution in Europe and the length of those contracts, the contracts in places like Australia".

The privatised company would need a new chairman, for the BL board was adamant that Horrocks could not continue in the position after the flotation. But it was argued that Egan was not the right person to replace him, because he did not have a track record that would sufficiently impress the City. "I set to, to look for a chairman who was acceptable to the banks, the City, the board, the DTI and, more importantly, to John Egan himself," Horrocks explains, "because there was absolutely no point in imposing somebody on John." Eventually, Horrocks suggested

Hamish Orr-Ewing, at that time chairman of Rank Xerox. Orr-Ewing had spent several years in the motor industry. In the 1960s, he had been product planning manager on the first Ford Cortina before doing a spell at BLMC. He joined Rank Xerox in 1965 and worked his way up through the company. An amateur engineer with an extremely well-equipped workshop at his home, Orr-Ewing was a Jaguar enthusiast and owned an E-Type.

He is very clear about why BL approached him to take on the Jaguar chairmanship, describing himself as "a reasonably well known member of the second eleven" among industrial managers; no one in the "first eleven" would have wanted the job during privatisation, he says. Orr-Ewing maintains that his appointment was always seen as transitory although no one discussed how long it was to last. He admired the way Egan had set up his management teams so as to ensure product quality, and had already met him some time before, to seek his advice on a refinement of management structure at Rank Xerox. Once he had been invited to take over as Jaguar chairman, the two met again and appeared to get on reasonably well.

Egan appears to have accepted the situation with equanimity. "That was one of the rules, one of the ideas at the time of privatisation," he says. "If I had to accept it, then I was willing to accept it." Orr-Ewing's appointment to the Jaguar Board was made in May 1984, and he took over as chairman on July 26. Ted Bond also joined the board in May, to strengthen the company's financial side. Edwards was clearly doing a good job, but it was felt necessary to bring in someone who would carry more weight with the City. Bond, according to Horrocks, was recommended by Hill Samuel; he had been finance director of the Beecham Group since 1972. Once the new directors were in place, the government announced that Jaguar was to be floated in July.

Relations between Jaguar and BL appear to have become steadily more difficult in the following weeks. Horrocks, being on both boards, came under pressure from both sides. The BL board, which saw Jaguar as a BL asset being sold, wanted the issuing price of Jaguar shares to be set as high as possible. It also wanted a slice of the profits that Jaguar had been earning. Jaguar's attitude was, naturally, quite different. It wanted the lowest possible share price in order to ensure a successful flotation, and the lowest level of debt that it could persuade the BL Board to agree. Senior managers at Jaguar had to cope with the dual task of helping to prepare for flotation and running the company. As assistant managing director Beasley puts it: "We'd get involved in some of the meetings and some of the efforts towards privatisation, but we tried to avoid putting that workload on to our people, because they had a full-time job in getting Series III right and developing XJ40."

Ken Edwards and John Edwards were, between them, responsible for preparing the reports on which to base the offer for sale document. Every single fact had to be verified. The reports mentioned Jaguar's success at Le Mans in the 1950s. "Then you have to prove it," Neil Johnson comments. "Everyone knows we won Le Mans, but finding a piece of paper which says you did . . ." After many hours of painstaking work, the offer for sale document was finished on July 2. "We learnt afterwards that heart attacks are commonplace during flotations," Johnson says. "Possibly the relative youth of the Jaguar Cars board was on our side at the time."

The offer for sale was issued as soon as finished, although the share price would not be announced for some time. In the second and third weeks of July, Orr-Ewing, Egan, John Edwards and David Boole began a promotional tour around stockbrokers. Edwards had mixed feelings about the tour because Jaguar was, to all intents and purposes, being sold by BL. This was one of the many sources of friction between Jaguar and the BL board. Edwards explains: "We thought, if BL are selling it, they should do the selling. Why should we go in and promote the sale price? But effectively, there was no one at BL who could sell . . . We were the offer, and we had to go and promote the sale of it."

Boole, of course, handled press relations. Having learnt his craft in various parts of BL, he was recognised as a talented PR man with experience of the financial community. He says,

"Although we didn't have much involvement with stockbrokers' analysts and so on, we did have quite a lot of contact with the financial media, so I knew most of them from the 1970s and I'd kept in touch with them." The only Jaguar director with direct experience of running a public company was Ken Edwards, who had been on the board of Pressed Steel 20 years before. Opinions vary on the degree to which the team was prepared for privatisation. Some maintain that the individuals concerned came to understand the nature of the transition only slowly. Others, mainly at Jaguar itself, claim that they were well able to cope with the changes.

While Browns Lane was the scene of frenzied activity in the run-up to the share-sale, a report appeared in the *Birmingham Post* under the headline, "Workers and council plan Jaguar bid". It claimed that a consortium was being put together, made up of Jaguar shop stewards, West Midlands County Council "and other local authorities", to acquire a 10 to 15 per cent stake in Jaguar. The inference was that the Jaguar men were in sympathy with the county council's hostility to the privatisation. The *Post* is published in the morning; its sister paper, the *Birmingham Evening Mail*, reaches the streets later in the day. A few hours after the story appeared in the *Post*, the *Evening Mail* reported that the shop stewards denied any involvement in the consortium – although they were, officially, opposed to the privatisation. They must, however, have been fairly lonely voices within Jaguar plants.

Egan maintains that attempts were made to find dissenting voices. "When we were being privatised, lots of people went in to find anybody who didn't want it to happen and I don't think they could find anybody," he claims. That is hardly surprising, for two reasons. A high proportion of the employees had experienced the attempts in earlier years to strip Jaguar of its identity, and the crippling damage to morale that they had brought. For that reason alone, many were certainly glad that the link with BL was to be severed. The privatisation also brought each employee a windfall in the shape of an allocation of shares. Egan was quoted in the *Post* as saying: "We think this is the best employee share scheme there is. What I wanted was for every employee to have a bag of money at the end of the day, as well as his or her salary and pension."

The sale had been scheduled for July, but it slipped into August. "It went through a very difficult patch, because in July, it was all off and on," John Edwards recalls. "This, again, made us think that the BL Board were a bit reluctant." The offer finally went ahead in August; the final date for applications was August 3. The price was fixed at 165 pence a share, which the *Financial Times* reported as being ". . . at least 10p to 15p below the forecasts of investment analysts". There were chaotic scenes at the new issues department of Barclays Bank in London's Farringdon Road, where share applications had to be lodged. The following day, newspapers reported that the price was expected to rise to 200 pence when dealing started the following Thursday. Needless to say, the scramble for shares led to opposition claims that the government had set the price too low, and had passed up a profit opportunity. Those who made these claims were apparently unaware that the money was to go to BL, not the government.

On Monday, August 6, it was announced that 320,000 valid applications had been received for shares. The offer was over-subscribed 8.3 times. This brought around £2.4 billion into BL's bank account and, according to Alison Hogan, writing in the *Financial Times*, the money earned BL £300,000 a night in interest. The volume of applications, however, meant that the first day of trading was put back from the following Thursday to the Friday. By now, it was rumoured that the opening share price would be more than 200 pence a share. Such forecasts were fuelled by the fact that the stock market had risen by around 8 per cent since the announcement of the issuing price of Jaguar shares; at the same time, the dollar was strengthening against the pound. In fact, the shares opened at a premium of only 11 pence when dealings began on August 10.

It is estimated that about 25 per cent of the company's 178 million shares changed hands on that first day of trading, with the price reaching a high of 181 pence. It closed at 179 pence, amid forecasts that heavy trading would continue the following week.

At Jaguar, according to Neil Johnson, there was an instant sense of euphoria. "The flotation had been a great success. The great band wagon was rolling. The media were on our side. But, in a detailed sense, I think it just meant that people felt more responsible, more accountable for what they were doing."

CHAPTER 10

A New Era of XJ Excellence

It is almost impossible to establish when a new car begins to take form. Stylists, engineers, product planners, marketing people will begin to daydream about a possible model long before any formal programme is defined. That was certainly true of the new Jaguar saloon, code named XJ40. Work had begun on the car even before the launch of the Series III XJ6 which it was to replace. Perhaps the most emotive aspect of a new car is its appearance. Although styling alone is usually insufficient to generate sales, it can lead potential customers to reject a car simply because they do not like the way it looks. That was one of Jaguar's biggest difficulties in the early development stages of the XJ40.

Ever since the company had begun building cars, the styling work had been done by William Lyons himself. He worked with craftsmen, directing them on how a panel was to be changed here, a highlight added or a line modified there. While Lyons was undoubtedly a styling genius, his domination of this aspect of the company's activities meant that, when he retired, there was no real successor. There was a small styling department, but the people within it had limited experience. One result is that an extraordinary number of individuals and outside studios seem to have tried to produce an acceptable design for the XJ40. Apart from the company's own staff, including engineering chief Bob Knight, the Italian design houses of Pininfarina, Bertone and Ital Design all had a crack at it. Work began at the beginning of the 1970s. The first quarter-scale model was finished in 1972 and the full size, fibre-glass model that was finally approved appeared some time in 1980.

Throughout this long period of development, Jaguar was conscious that the XJ40 had to be evolutionary. The market for which it was destined does not like radical change. New offerings from

Mercedes and BMW, too, are refinements of existing products, rather than stylistic trail-blazers, despite the fact that the failure of a new model would not be catastrophic for either, in the sense of threatening the company with extinction. For Jaguar, circumstances were very different. The XJ40 was destined to replace the model that took around 80 per cent of the company's sales. If the market did not like it, the company was doomed. There is little doubt that that was one of the reasons why Jaguar eventually opted for rather conservative styling.

It took time to reach that conclusion, partly because, between 1970 and 1980, the company had a series of different masters, all of whom wanted to influence the design. So it is scarcely surprising that the photographs of the various styling exercises suggest that Jaguar spent the 1970s desperately casting around for a style that would carry it through to the 1990s. The search took it down some peculiar avenues. Once a body style is approved within the company, it is necessary to find out whether the car buying public agrees with the stylists. Today, this is normally done by means of styling clinics or hall tests. The process is time-consuming and expensive, so the aim is to obtain as much information as possible.

Security is crucial. It must be possible to seal off the hall used for the test, because the car is probably still some years away from launch. Not even the identity of the manufacturer is disclosed to the people brought in to give their opinions. The new car is displayed alongside its prime competition; in Jaguar's case, that includes Mercedes, BMW and, in America, Cadillac. The relevant existing model is also included for comparison purposes. All the cars have, as far as possible, the same standard of finish, they are usually the same colour and all identifying badges are removed.

The people whose views are sought are carefully selected. Some are existing owners; some own a competing model; some are not yet able to afford the types of cars on display but are likely to be able to in the near future. All undergo a programme designed to find out exactly what they think of each of the cars on show and, particularly, how the new car compares with the competition.

Joe Greenwell, of Jaguar's sales and marketing department, was responsible for some of the later XJ40 clinics. He says the time taken to complete the programme varies widely. "Some people could be through in two and a half hours, some will be there for eight." That can cause difficulties in New York, where people tend to be rushing to their next appointment. Los Angeles and Britain, however, are different. "In the UK, people love to talk about Jaguars and also, there's a tremendous excitement in seeing something new that you know not many other people will have seen. That generally puts you ahead of the game. People will want to stay and so we manage to get a lot of information."

That comment highlights one inescapable fact: although respondents were not supposed to know the provenance of the new car, it was so clearly a development of the existing Series III that the manufacturer was easily identifiable. Indeed, one of the objectives of the clinic was to see if the car was recognisably a Jaguar. "At no stage do you tell them what it is," Greenwell says, "but in the Jaguar hall test, you're wasting your time because that's part of the magic. We have a house style that is instantly recognisable. It's part of our marketing task to ensure that the house style doesn't need a back-up."

The first tests were used to confirm that the style was right, so that work could progress in the knowledge that the basic bodyshell would not change. That stage, known as signing off the body in white, in other words, approving the bare metal shell, was the moment at which Jaguar began to commit serious money to the project. BL's appproval was needed; and the board was asked to approve funds for the development of XJ40 in July 1980.

Chief engineer Jim Randle says BL's quality man, Charles Maple, gave considerable help. "When we put XJ40 forward, we had to produce a detailed account of where the car was in terms of its development programme. A lot of people thought we hadn't done much work, but in fact, we'd done quite a lot. Charles did a lot of lobbying with the BL board at that time to help us through." It ought to have been obvious that a considerable amount of work had been done, because the UK launch date for the car was shown in the submission as autumn 1983, with launches in export markets in the spring of 1984. That left only three years.

Once the body had been signed off, it was passed to the body engineers, who had to work out how to build it. In the past, this had been one of Jaguar's worst failings. Lyons designed beautiful cars, but they were a nightmare for the body engineers. Some claim, too, that pressure was put on the engineers to use smaller panels because the tools needed to make them were cheaper. Under Egan, the rules were different; the XJ40 body eventually used 425 panels, compared with 584 for Series III. "We looked for methods of body construction that involved fewer panels," Beasley recalls. "Fewer mashed together and sculpted panels, fewer spotwelds to maintain the integrity of the bodyshell." The aim was a bodyshell that was cheaper to produce and that could be built to more consistent quality standards. The stylists had already eliminated some pitfalls by omitting various difficult styling features of the Series I, II and III, such as the "sculpting" around the headlights.

Executives responsible for the manufacturing side made their wishes known in other areas. This was a crucial development for Jaguar. In the past, a car had been designed and manufacturing told to built it. That had caused some of the poor quality that had plagued the company over the years. If a car is not designed to be easy to build, the chances of it being reliable are significantly reduced. Manufacturing chief Mike Beasley drew up what he refers to as "wants lists". "We identified features that we felt were desirable from a 'design to make' point of view," he says. One such was the ability to "body drop", that is, install the engine from below the car during the assembly process. On Series III, engines had to be lowered into the engine bay from above. That increased the risk of damage to the paintwork on the wings.

New equipment in the manufacturing areas was high on the wants list. "Some of the facilities that we used to build the XK engine were very well amortised," he says. "I'm sure Noah used some of them to put his ark together. We got some newer kit in there, and we've put in a lot more since. The result, again, has been fewer man hours, a lot more quality, integrity, designed into the product."

Beasley admits that the manufacturing team did miss one opportunity. "We didn't go for door-off assembly. That was a tragic mistake that we'll get to shortly." This is a technique that is now used in some volume car plants and involves taking the doors off a body once it has been painted and mounting them on some form of separate carrier. This provides more space for assembly line workers to get in and out of the cars and reduces the risk of damage to the doors. At the end of the track, the doors are mated with the body again. But perhaps the biggest mistake of all was made not by manufacturing but by a combination of the BLEO marketing department and Jaguar's engineering department.

Towards the end of the 1970s, BLEO concluded that the V12 engine had no future. It maintained that the rising cost of petrol would make such a thirsty engine unattractive to car buyers in the 1980s. There would, therefore, be no need for a V12 version of the XJ40. The message was relayed to Jaguar engineering, which was fighting to keep the AJ6 engine project alive in the face of suggestions from the BL board that the Rover V8 engine should be used instead. Under different circumstances, the designers would probably have retained enough space to make a V12 variant an option. In fact, engineering grasped the opportunity presented by BLEO, and designed the XJ40 engine bay so that a V-shaped engine could not be fitted into it. That ruled out the Rover V8 – but also a Jaguar-designed V12. Engineering director Jim Randle was then able to write a paper explaining that, if the Rover engine was to be used, the front of the car would have to be re-designed. Now, because a V12 variant is so obviously necessary, the XJ40 engine bay is having to be extensively re-engineered to take such an engine, and the current V12 is still fitted in the old body.

Battles with the BL board were far from being Randle's only handicap. In 1980, he could only spare 13 engineers to work on XJ40. Most of his staff were needed to correct faults in the current car. Coping with both jobs was "a crazy thing to do now that I look at it", Randle says. The situation was partly brought about by Egan, who placed the emphasis firmly on improving Series III. Randle recognises that if that decision had not been taken, Jaguar would probably have gone out of business. In 1980, sales of the Series III were falling, partly because of supply shortfalls, partly because of poor quality and reliability. Had that trend been allowed to continue, the reputation of the company would not have recovered in time for the introduction of the new car and the profits that were earned from 1982 would not have been there.

The fact remains that resources were insufficient to continue developing XJ40 at the time, and the magnitude of the task had probably not been fully appreciated anyway. Randle points out that the British motor industry had developed few completely new cars in the decades since the second world war (one of them had been the Rover 2000). It was a case of ignorance being bliss. As Randle now says, "In truth, there was no way, with the resources we'd got, that we would ever have got it ready, had we had sufficient foresight to see the size of the problem we were tackling. With the benefit of hindsight, I don't think I'd ever try to do such a thing again."

An attempt was made to take some of the difficulties out of launching a completely new car by introducing the AJ6 engine into the XJ-S. This happened in October 1983 and was a continuance of another Jaguar tradition. When the XK engine was being developed for the 1950s saloon cars, it was first tried out on the motoring public in the XK120 sports car. The AJ6 received a very different reaction to the XK, however. Randle puts it bluntly: "We got clobbered. Again, you see, we set out to do something that nobody else could, apparently, do. We tried to make an in-line, aluminium six. There isn't another aluminium six in production and there isn't because they're hard, very hard."

The AJ6 did not compare well with the V12 that had been fitted to the XJ-S. It was not the smooth, quiet, sophisticated power unit expected of Jaguar. Randle explains: "We had to learn things about engines that we didn't know. We learnt, for example, that putting six-cylinder cranks into big, cast iron blocks disguises problems." The difficulties come to light only when those cranks are installed in light aluminium blocks. It took a long time to bring the AJ6 to an acceptable standard, but Randle stresses that the engine is now reliable. By the end of 1987, around 30,000 had been produced and only four, he says, had needed to be replaced. "One of those, incidentally, had the wrong plugs in."

Joe Greenwell joined Jaguar's new sales and marketing department in January, 1983, and immediately began to plan a series of clinics for the XJ40. These took place during 1984 in New York and at Sandown Park in Britain; some work was also done in West Germany. By this time, the company had already missed the original 1983 launch deadline and was soon to miss the second and the third.

"We got cars going down the track at the time we said we were going to do it," Randle recalls, "but I think they would have put us out of business pretty damn quick if we'd tried to sell them." Fortunately, sales of the Series III were climbing and the pressure to replace it was easing. "We kept asking ourselves, 'Why are we doing this? We have a product here that's rapidly becoming a cult car and here we are trying to get rid of it.' So we put the launch off," Randle says. The first proposed launch date was probably something of a fiction anyway, devised to persuade the BL board to release funds for the car. It was achievable, just, if everything went perfectly, first time, but people at Browns Lane must have known that 1983 was never a realistic proposition. However, after they had put off the launch date once, it seemed to become a habit.

The second missed date appeared in a paper written in 1982, presenting a marketing strategy for the period from 1983 to 1987. This assumed that XJ40 would be unveiled at the Geneva Motor Show in March 1984; the car's UK launch would take place at the same time and deliveries to Europe would begin in the autumn. By the time Derek Waeland appeared on the scene as XJ40 project director in early 1983, March 1984 had given way to autumn 1984 as the launch target. In an interview published in *Car* magazine to coincide with the actual launch of the XJ40 in October 1986, Waeland recalled the lack of new manufacturing facilities. "I was . . . amazed, when I came in '83, that the proposed launch date was October '84. I said there was no way." Part of the marketing team's plan for the launch of the car involved rebuilding the front of the Browns Lane offices to include a theatre that could be used for conferences. The work was put in hand in December 1983; Peter Battam still expected the launch to take

place in October 1984. Had he known that it would be delayed
for a further two years, he would have installed considerably more
sophisticated facilities in the theatre.

Joe Greenwell's clinic work was also based on the belief that
the launch would be in October 1984. The clinics, however,
contributed to the decision to postpone it, for the response to the
car's interior was less than enthusiastic. "We had designed a car
to a specification which, I suppose, matched a BMW 7 Series type
of concept rather than a Series III concept," Greenwell says.
"We'd walked away from traditional materials – wood, chrome
and leather." That might not have mattered too much had the
work been well executed, but it was not. Neil Johnson was
involved in approving the original work; he maintains that part
of the difficulty stemmed from a lack of experience. He admits
that he found it hard to recognise when he was being shown a
hand finished item that would look much better in final form and
when he was being misled.

He explains: "When you're looking at a mock-up of an ash
tray, for example, and somebody tells you, 'Of course, this looks
awful, but the real thing will be beautiful' . . . you really want to
believe him. The reality is you can't, and you have to say, 'I don't
believe you. Show me.' Until he satisfies you that it is right, you
must never tick it off the list of things to do.

"Too many things got ticked off with people saying, 'That's the
concept. Don't, please, take this as what it will look like because
it will be super. That's the way it will work. That's where it will
be. That's the colour it will be.' And you would say, terrific, well
done. Then six or 12 months later, you come back to the car for
a styling review and you see a production prototype of this
Leonardo-da-Vinci-designed piece of equipment actually fitted,
and you say, 'What is this?' And they say, 'Well, that's the ash
tray you signed off.' And you throw it at them. I mention ash
trays because they were one of the things that were in that
category."

According to Johnson, several people warned that the interior
was not right, and their misgivings were confirmed by the results
of the clinics. Greenwell reports that the UK clinic gave "a shot

across the bows". The response to the interior was unfavourable. So he watched the American clinic results with heightened interest. He suspected that if potential British customers were concerned about the lack of traditional Jaguar interior finishes, the Americans were likely to be even more critical. They were.

The American clinic supported the findings of those in the UK and Germany; there was a general demand for the reinstatement of features judged to represent the traditional British approach. "They wanted some wood back in," Greenwell says, "they wanted some chrome back in, they wanted some leather back in." He points out that leather had been removed only from the bottom of the range car, and strongly denies rumours that the results of the American clinics were a disaster. "What you had were a series of indications," he says. "I don't think they would have affected the basic success of the product worldwide. I think we would have been under pressure to do what we actually did if we had launched the car . . . to put some Jaguar values back into it."

Greenwell's view that the car's success would not have been jeopardised by the interior is open to question. A fundamental aspect of the approach that had been adopted was that the European interior, as it was called, made the XJ40 a more direct competitor to its BMW and Mercedes equivalents. Yet it could be argued that one of the reasons for Series III's success was that it did not compete head-on with the German cars. It had something that set it apart from them. That something was the softer, more comfortable interior. The Americans certainly seemed to prefer the softer approach.

When Greenwell returned from America, he was called in to see Egan. He reported that the XJ40 was seen as a worthy successor to the XJ6, but it needed some further work on the interior. "Trim enhancement is how it came to be termed," Greenwell says.

The cars were put through another series of clinics in July 1986 to make sure that the revised interior was what customers wanted. It passed the test.

So the combination of buoyant Series III sales and the need for further development work on XJ40 meant that the launch date slipped yet again. This time, however, Jaguar did the job properly and put it back to 1986. Roger Putnam, sales operations director, refused to quote a launch date when he spoke to dealers in 1984. "The XJ40 will appear when the car is ready, when we're ready and when you're ready," he told them. He admits that, at the time, the delay was "quite a jolt", but maintains that the extra time was invaluable since it meant that the quality of the dealer network could be further improved by the time the car was launched. He believes the dealers would have coped had the slippage not occurred, although he would probably have had to use XJ40 allocations to persuade some of them to come up to standard. "There are all sorts of things we could have done had the car been launched earlier," he says, "but it was nice to do it in a more leisurely and friendly way, rather than continually beating the drum and sabre rattling."

The delay enabled the engineering team to extend the testing programme well beyond anything that Jaguar had attempted before. It was just as well. Series III, in its early years, had displayed tell-tale signs of insufficient testing and development. Moreover, when the XJ40 was being planned, Jaguar had none of the rig testing equipment that is now an essential part of a modern car manufacturing company. By the time the car was finally launched, it was in place.

A test base was set up in an industrial estate on the outskirts of Phoenix, Arizona. From there, cars were driven over three designated routes, clocking up around 700 miles a day, every weekday. The routes took in both tough mountain roads and desert stretches where temperatures rise to near the American summer maximum. In total, the test cars at Phoenix covered around 1.5 million miles. About 1.2 million miles of winter testing, in sub-zero temperatures, were done from a centre near Timmins, Ontario. Further tests were carried out near Cobar, 600 miles north-west of Sydney, and in Oman; and high-speed trials took place on the Nardo circuit, in southern Italy. All this was in addition to testing in less remote locations. The whole programme included some 5.5 million miles of driving. Rigs in the factory were used to find out weaknesses in components.

Throughout the period of development, the question of what to call the car repeatedly came up for discussion. Apart from the original use of the Jaguar name by SS Cars to denote a specific model, the company had never used names. Johnson recalls that when he arrived in 1982, the designations 290 and 360 – indicating engine sizes – were in use. He did not feel they were the right solution; nor did he believe the company should break with tradition and give the car a name, though lists of possibilities were circulated. It was generally considered that to call the XJ40 Series IV would suggest that there had been little more than a facelift. In the end, the XJ6 designation was retained. (In this book, however, the car is referred to consistently as the XJ40, to avoid confusion with Series III.)

A new car is launched, today, in several stages. Most manufacturers first show it to selected motoring journalists, and provide them with an opportunity to drive it. That normally happens several weeks before the public first sees the car, to encourage magazines to feature it on their front covers. The second group to see the car are the company's dealers. They will be brought to a central location for a show that owes more to theatre than to the motor industry. Again, this will usually happen several weeks before the public announcement, so the dealers can prepare their launch activities. Fleet customers will follow the dealers; a variation of the dealers' show will normally be provided for them. These are the people who buy cars for police forces, large companies, leasing companies and local authorities. They are increasingly important in the industry because they buy around half of all new cars sold. For Jaguar, they are even more crucial, for only around 20 per cent of Jaguars are sold to private customers.

Finally, the car is announced to the public, usually in the middle of the week and often at one of the motor shows. Jaguar followed this formula for the XJ40, but it added two extra elements: presentations to the City of London and to its own employees. Much of this programme was co-ordinated by Battam's department. "It really got serious about 10 months out," he says. A detailed marketing platform was worked out by Greenwell's team, and was used to brief F. John French, Jaguar's advertising agency, and Cricket Communications, of Birmingham, the company that was going to handle some of the launch presentations. The platform, divided into several sections, was written during December 1985 and was based on information received from the clinics. In general, such documents tend to shy away from realism. Austin Rover, for instance, has frequently listed, as product benefits, such styling features as side stripes. The marketing platform can, in fact, easily become an exercise in internal hype. Whether this was the case with the XJ40 platform it is impossible to say, since it remains a secret. It set out expected sales volumes, where customers were likely to be found and how many it was hoped to tempt away from Mercedes and BMW. The document also included marketing strategies for challenging the Ford Scorpio, the Rover 800, Volvos, Audis and Saabs.

This was, perhaps, the most important aspect of the plan. Jaguar had recognised that the only way to achieve growth was by winning business from other makers of executive-level cars. For that reason, it set a base price of £16,495. The Rover Sterling was due to be launched later that same year and, although the Jaguar strategists could not have known it at the time, the XJ40 would undercut the Rover by £2,300. It also undercut the Ford Scorpio. This aggressive pricing policy by Egan and his team harked back to an earlier era in the company's history. William Lyons had often caused consternation among competitors by employing such tactics. But the announcement of prices was still a long way off when Battam received the marketing platform and began to discuss advertising strategy with F. John French.

The story that had to be communicated was complex, and the agency began to develop advertising concepts for three separate cars – the XJ6, the Sovereign and the Daimler – to a broad spectrum of potential customers. It is a measure of the nervousness with which the launch was approached, that around 200 visuals were produced and researched. Battam says the result was, to say the least, confusing. "We'd researched just about every conceivable thing. We'd researched the length of copy; how aggressive we could be with the XJ6 range – not knocking, but nevertheless, aggressive; how to position the Sovereign above the XJ6 range;

where the Daimler fitted into the overall mix." What emerged from this mountain of information? In Battam's words: "They want a nice big hero shot of the car; the car's got to look beautiful, with short copy and a headline that makes sense. Which is something we all knew 10 months before."

Photography causes difficulties at all launches. There never seem to be enough cars for all the people who need them, and the photographs have to be taken in complete secrecy. Some manufacturers insist that photographers and their staff sign undertakings to maintain confidentiality. Some insist that all film is processed by the company taking the photographs. Cars are moved around the country in covered transporters and when the transporter cannot get close to a studio, the cars have to be kept covered with a dust sheet while they are manoeuvred.

With the XJ40 it was no different. Special camouflage was developed for the road test cars, and it was reported that even people who worked in the test centres had no idea what the "naked" cars looked like. But Jaguar did take a risk in August, 1986, when Jim Randle and his engineering colleagues presented the story of the engineering and development of the XJ40 at the Institution of Mechanical Engineers, in London. Randle decided that he wanted to show the car to the members of the institution. The difficulty was getting the car into the building through the narrow main doorway and then into the lecture hall. The feat was accomplished with the help of a specially designed trolley with a cradle that could rotate the car on to its side.

Tricky as it was to get the car in and out, the exercise appears to have escaped the attentions of the press. The question of security has become a battle between the motoring magazines, notably *Car*, and the manufacturers. *Car* prides itself on carrying photographs of cars that have not yet been launched. It seems not to matter that the photographs often give only a vague impression of the new car. In August 1985, the magazine triumphantly announced: "After nearly two years of trying, we present the first undisguised views of Jaguar's new luxury saloon, the XJ40, due on our roads in 1987." The accompanying shots were of poor quality. In March, 1986, however, *Car* breached the security screen again. This time, the photographs were good quality, colour shots.

Communications chief David Boole admits that car manufacturers can become over-cautious about photographs of their new products appearing in magazines. "Don't forget, the XJ40 was perhaps the most anticipated car ever in the British motor industry. People were talking about it left, right and centre and we thought that under those circumstances, it was necessary to preserve as much mystique as we could until the end." The company carried out investigations to try and find out how *Car* had obtained the photographs, but never managed to track down the source.

When the XJ40 was finally unveiled to the public, Jaguar placed only 17 advertisements, and only one of those was in a national daily newspaper: the *Financial Times*. Only two different advertisements were run – one for the XJ6 and one for the Sovereign. There was no advertisement for the Daimler and yet, within a year, it was responsible for 30 per cent of range sales. Talking a year after the launch, Battam said, "Those two together totalled 17 insertions which finished at the end of November, and we've never advertised the car since. It was the most important car launch that I've ever been involved in, but in terms of financial expenditure, it was certainly the tiniest."

Judging by the space that was booked, and estimating the cost of producing the advertisements, it seems likely that Jaguar spent around £250,000 on its launch advertising. When BMW launched its new 7 Series in 1987, it was rumoured to have spent more than £3 million on advertising in Britain alone. Apart from the fact that Jaguar lacks the resources of bigger companies, its frugal approach reflected a successful gamble on the level of media interest in the launch. Boole was responsible for generating media coverage, so he obviously influenced the decision on advertising. "Clearly the launch was going to attract a lot of press coverage, so I said that while it was prudent to do some advertising, a lot of advertising at the time of launch would be superfluous." The main thrust of the public relations was in September, when the press previews took place. Boole was responsible for organising these and must have experienced an occasional feeling of *déjà vu*.

In 1980, he had been working at BLEO and was responsible for the press launch of the Austin Metro. Although the Metro and the XJ40 might seem totally dissimilar, they have some common features. Both are British-built, and the Britishness of each was judged to be an important part of the launch. The Metro's launch was the occasion for a display of rampant chauvinism; there was none of that at the XJ40 launch, but the venues chosen for it were British when the industry norm is to use exotic, overseas locations. A second common element was the importance of the two cars to the companies building them. In 1980, it was said that the Metro would not ensure the survival of BL, but if it failed, then the chances were that BL would fail too. With XJ40, the stakes were even higher. So Boole has the distinction of having been responsible for the press launches of two great white hopes for two very different companies.

Boole explains his choice of venue for the press launch by pointing out that most UK companies follow a fairly standard format. "They tend to go abroad, for major launches anyway. We wanted to do something different." He and his team spent months searching for the right venue and eventually found it in the Stakis Dunkeld hotel, Tayside. Jaguar took over the hotel for a month and brought in journalists from the UK, Europe, Australia, the US and Canada. While those presentations were in progress, the theatre at Browns Lane was in daily use for groups of dealers; shortly afterwards, attention moved to the National Exhibition Centre, between Coventry and Birmingham.

During the works shutdown in September, the company took over the Forum, one of the giant exhibition halls at the exhibition centre, for what amounted to a launch of the car to employees and their families. These were known as the J Days and used the special mechanism that had been built to reveal the car to the dealers at Browns Lane. All employees received invitations to attend one of the four days of the event with their families. They were received in groups of 250, a group arriving every 45 minutes. After a speech from one of the directors and the presentation of the car, they moved out to see the displays in the hall. Each department had produced a section of the exhibition to show its contribution to the new car. Mike Kinsky was responsible for the event. "That was the culmination of what Hearts and Minds is all about," he says, referring to the company's programme to involve employees in the business.

Once the J Days were over, Battam and Cricket Communications had 24 hours to move the "reveal" mechanism, all 20 tons of it, to London's Park Lane Hilton, for a special launch for the City. Battam had known that the schedule for the move was tight, but he did not know how tight. "We did it with about eight minutes to spare," he says.

All that remained was to announce the new car to the public. In choosing precisely when to do that, Boole recalled his experience with the Metro, when he had succeeded in getting two bursts of press interest by unveiling the car at the Paris motor show a week before the British motor show. "I made sure we did exactly the same thing with XJ40."

On October 7, dealers all over Britain held celebration launch night parties, and someone from the company was sent to speak at every one. The dealers had been provided with a briefing document as part of the Jaguar Contact service. This included background information on the car, an explanation of the marketing platform, details of the advertising campaign and advice on how the dealer should go about launching the car locally. Local press advertisements, direct mail leaflets, invitations and display units were provided, although some items were quite expensive.

A film about the development of the car was also offered. A film crew had travelled all over the world to gather footage, but Battam realised that nowhere was there a clear shot of the car. "It was always under disguise, and the only place where we'd got permission to go and film the car was on top of a Welsh mountain," he says. "The weather was as it can only be on the top of Welsh mountains, but nobody spotted us filming, because nobody in his right mind is on top of a Welsh mountain in that sort of weather."

Immediately after launch, waiting lists built up across the country and by the time the advertising finished at the end of November, customers were being told that they would have to wait between nine months and a year for delivery. That partly explains why the car was not advertised during the year following the launch. "If you start advertising too early in the game, all you do is upset customers and dealers," Battam says. "On the other hand, you can't leave it until the waiting list evaporates." It is vital to choose the right moment.

The development costs of the XJ40 have been put at around £200 million, a paltry sum by motor industry standards. The Mercedes 190 Series is reckoned to have cost £500 million, but the XJ40's success seems to have been unaffected by its relatively low costs.

The car marked a milestone in Jaguar's development under its new management, although much of the development work was carried out before John Egan arrived at Browns Lane. The likelihood must be that, had it not been for the Egan team's tough and uncompromising approach, the XJ40 would have been yet another Jaguar brilliantly conceived but indifferently executed.

The XJ40 was far from perfect when it was launched, and there is clearly some disappointment in the company that flaws have appeared. But perhaps the most remarkable thing about these faults is not that they happened but that they did not damage Jaguar's reputation. Nothing better illustrates the differences between Jaguar in the 1970s and Jaguar today.

CONCLUSION

The 20 years that elapsed between the formation of British Motor Holdings and the launch of the XJ40 are merely an episode in Jaguar's history. Nothing is finished. The company is on its way back, but it still has far to go before it will be possible to say that recovery is complete. Nevertheless, the management team at Browns Lane can without a doubt congratulate itself on its achievements so far. It is unlikely to spend much time doing that, because it knows that the next few years will be even tougher than the last seven.

At the beginning of 1988, the dollar was again weak, but the company said it would not be too badly affected because it had forward dollar exchange contracts for the next 12 months. Some executives were, however, privately expressing concern. Jaguar is more dependent on the American market than ever before. Having said that, it seems unlikely that Sir John Egan and his team would be unable to cope, even if the pound became as grossly overvalued in the future as it was in 1980. Obviously profits would fall if that happened, but Jaguar seems fit enough to survive.

There is no doubt, however, that the company will be vulnerable once the "golden share" disappears at the end of 1990. Its very success in rebuilding its reputation is making it more attractive to predators, and there are several of those around. The big American automotive groups, in particular, have shown a desire to buy respected makers of high performance cars. General Motors now owns Lotus; Chrysler owns Lamborghini; Ford owns Aston Martin. Jaguar would be a very tempting proposition for any of them, and they would probably be prepared to pay more than the market price for it. It is, of course, also possible that a company not currently involved with the motor industry would be tempted. Any suitor is likely to be rebuffed.

Sir John Egan has one trump card. He and his senior team can say that they would not stay with Jaguar if it lost its independence. That ploy would undoubtedly have an effect, but in order for it to work, a majority of the shareholders has to be convinced that the future for Jaguar is better with Egan in the chair than with someone else. At the same time, it is in the company's interest that he should begin to bring forward a successor, so that when the time comes for him to move on, there can be a smooth transfer of power.

That, however, is probably a long time off yet. A more immediate focus of attention is the first car that will be a true product of the Egan team: the XJ41. This is being billed as a successor to the E-Type and although it was being discussed in the days of Jaguar-Rover-Triumph, the important decisions affecting its design had apparently not been taken when Egan arrived. By contrast, much of the work on the XJ40 had been completed by then, albeit by some of the people now regarded as part of the new management team.

The future holds fascinating questions and intriguing possibilities. For example, will Jaguar's new engineering centre at Whitley, near Coventry, be allowed to take on contract work as do both Lotus and Porsche? Judging from some comments, the idea is being considered in the front offices at Browns Lane. Perhaps it is a form of diversification that would be acceptable to the board.

The one absolutely clear fact is that Jaguar's recovery is not yet complete. As Egan puts it: "I've always been of the opinion that it was going to take a very long time to get the company turned round properly, because you're trying to be a world class competitor. You're trying to do some things better than anybody else in the world can do them. Don't be so naïve as to think that kind of design tradition and heritage gets built up in two minutes. It does not."

178

APPENDIX 1

JAGUAR PROFIT 1960 – 1967

Profit after tax

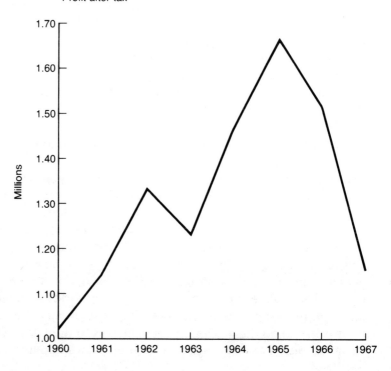

No separate figures were issued for Jaguar between 1967 and 1980. For figures from 1980, see Appendix 2.

APPENDIX 2

JAGUAR FINANCIAL RESULTS AND SALES 1980 – 1987

	Turnover £ millions	Profit (Loss) £ millions	Capital Expenditure £ millions	Employees in UK	Production	World Sales	UK Registrations
1980	166.4	(52.2)	7.7	9,210	13,791	15,469	5,920
1981	195.2	(36.3)	21.3	7,873	14,577	13,933	5,688
1982	305.6	6.5	38.8	7,518	22,046	21,007	6,440
1983	472.6	49.5	33.3	8,306	28,041	28,467	7,069
1984	634.1	42.6	38.1	9,500	33,437	32,956	7,544
1985	746.5	87.6	57.2	10,441	38,500	37,952	8,049
1986	830.4	83.4	93.9	11,324	41,437	41,256	7,579
1987	1,002.1	61.3	132.0	12,483	48,020	49,200	11,102

APPENDIX 3

**DOLLAR/POUND CURRENCY MOVEMENTS 1973–1987
(EXPRESSED AS DOLLARS TO £1.)**

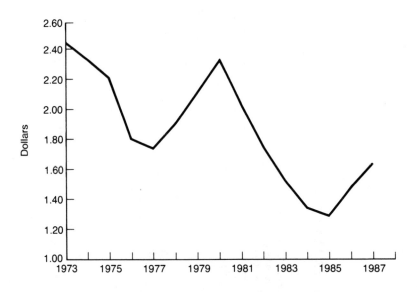

(*Source* – Extel.)

APPENDIX 4

**DOLLAR/POUND MOVEMENTS DURING THE CRUCIAL
1980/82 PERIOD, EXPRESSED AS DOLLARS TO £1.**

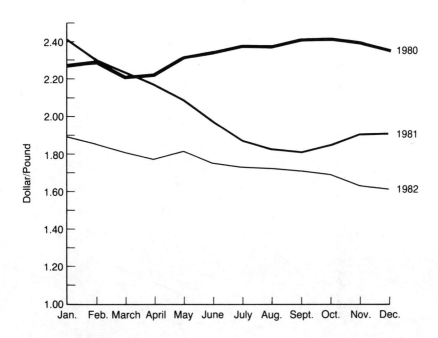

(*Source* – Central Statistical Office.)

APPENDIX 5

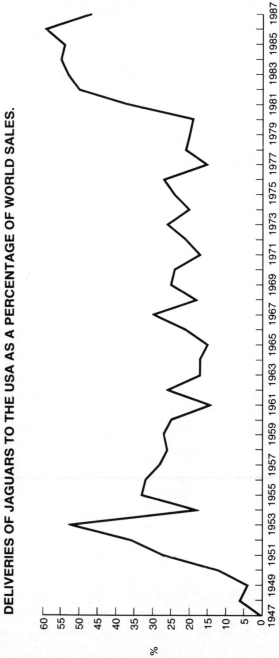

DELIVERIES OF JAGUARS TO THE USA AS A PERCENTAGE OF WORLD SALES.

APPENDIX 6

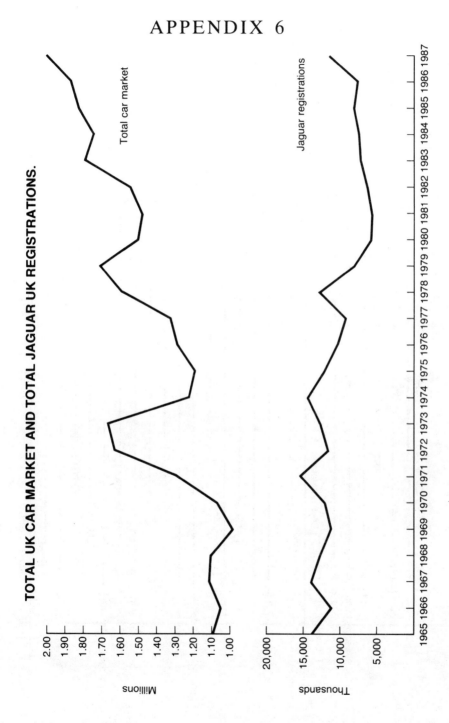

APPENDIX 7

COMPANY FORMATIONS AND MERGERS

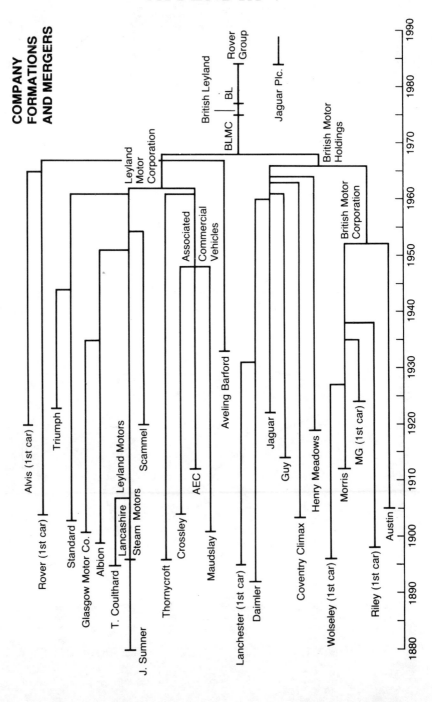

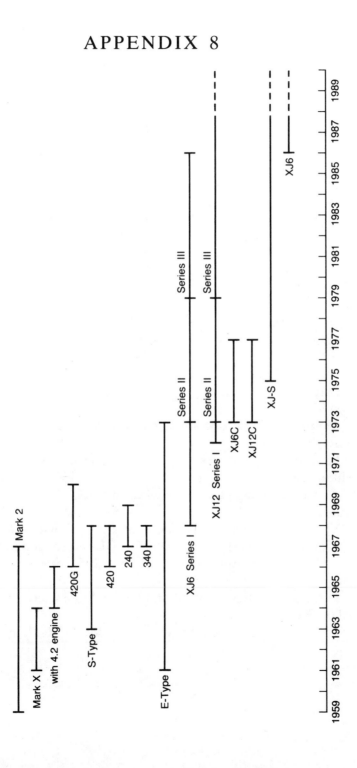

APPENDIX 8

185

JAGUAR NEW MODEL INTRODUCTIONS

Mark 2

Mark X

with 4.2 engine

420G

S-Type

420

240

340

E-Type

XJ6 Series I

Series II

Series III

XJ12 Series I

Series II

Series III

XJ6C

XJ12C

XJ-S

XJ6

1959 1961 1963 1965 1967 1969 1971 1973 1975 1977 1979 1981 1983 1985 1987 1989

APPENDIX 9

Cast of Characters

I would like to thank the following individuals for being so generous in helping me research the book. Their names and job titles are shown here in order to help follow the train of events that has been described.

However, it seems unecessary to include all the positions that they have held over the years which have nothing to do with Jaguar. Therefore, the dates shown relate only to periods when the individuals had some connection with the company. Where no dates are shown, the individuals concerned is currently holding that position.

David Andrews
    Main Board Director, BL Ltd, 1975–86
    Executive Vice Chairman, BL Ltd, 1978–82
Anthony Archer
    Director, Evans Halshaw Holdings Plc.
Tony Ball
    Chairman BL Europe and Overseas, 1979–82
Peter Battam
    Manager, World Marketing Services, Jaguar Cars
Mike Beasley
    Assistant Managing Director, Jaguar Cars
Bob Berry
    Various management positions in PR, publicity, sales operations and marketing for Jaguar, BL International, Leyland Cars and BL Europe and Overseas, 1951–80
David Boole
    Director, Communications and Public Affairs, Jaguar Cars
Alan Clark
    Chairman & Chief Executive, Collier Motor Holdings Ltd.

Tony Cusmano
General Manager, Rallye Motors, New Jersey
Joe Edwards
Managing Director, BMC, 1966–68
John Edwards
Director, Finance – Jaguar Cars
Ken Edwards
Director, Personnel and Company Secretary – Jaguar Cars
Sir John Egan
Chairman and Chief Executive, Jaguar Plc
Joe Greenwell
Manager, Product Affairs – Jaguar Cars
(Manager, Marketing & Product Research – Jaguar Cars, 1983–84)
Malcolm Hart
Various management positions within sales operations and
franchising for Standard Triumph, BLMC, Leyland Cars and
BLEO
Jonathan Heynes
Quality Operations Manager – Jaguar Cars
Ray Horrocks
Chairman & Managing Director, Austin Morris 1978–80
Managing Director, BL Cars, 1980–81
Chairman & Chief Executive, BL Cars Group 1981–82
Group Chief Executive, Cars (a division of BL) 1982–86
Executive Director & Board Member, BL Plc, 1981–86
Neil Johnson
Sales and Marketing Director – Jaguar Cars, 1982–86
Mike Kinsky
Director, Employee Relations – Jaguar Cars
Bob Knight
Engineering Director, Jaguar Cars, 1972–80
Managing Director, Jaguar Cars, 1978–80
Ron Lucas
Deputy Managing Director, BMC, 1965–66
Director of Finance, BMH, 1966–68
Main Board Director, BLMC, 1968–75
Main Board Director, British Leyland, 1975–77

Charles Maple,
  Quality Director, BLMC et seq, 1975–85
John Morgan
  Director, Continental European Operations – Jaguar Cars
Hamish Orr-Ewing
  Chairman, Jaguar Plc, 1984-85
Roger Putnam
  Director, Sales and Marketing – Jaguar Cars
Jim Randle
  Director, Product Engineering – Jaguar Cars
Geoffrey Robinson
  Chief Executive, Jaguar Cars, 1973–75
Cedric Scroggs
  Marketing Director, Leyland Cars, 1976–78
Lord Stokes
  Chairman & Managing Director, BLMC, 1968–75
  President, British Leyland, 1975–79
Trevor Taylor
  Sales Director, Leyland Cars and Austin Rover Group
Norman Tebbit
  Parliamentary Under Secretary of State, Department of Trade
    1979–81
Pratt Thompson
  Chairman, Jaguar Rover Triumph, 1978–79
Tony Thompson
  Responsible for Jaguar assembly plant, 1975–76
Ray Underwood
  Marketing Director, RTA Advertising
Graham Whitehead
  President, Jaguar Cars Inc.

Index

Index compiled by Peva Keane